Trade Works

Trade Works

Andreas Schweitzer

First edition published in the United States by Leaders Press © 2023.
This revised edition was published in 2025 by Andreas Schweitzer,
in partnership with Whitefox Publishing

www.wearewhitefox.com

Copyright © Andreas Schweitzer, 2025

EU GPSR Authorised Representative
LOGOS EUROPE, 9 rue Nicolas Poussin,
17000, LA ROCHELLE, France
E-mail: Contact@logoseurope.eu

ISBN 9781916797871
Also available as an eBook
ISBN 9781916797888

Proofread by Anne Downes
Designed and typeset by Couper Street Type Co.
Cover design by Tomás Almeida
Project management by Whitefox

To my family and in memory of our parents,
with gratitude and love

Contents

Trade . . . makes it possible for men to understand that they have common wants and must act in common to supply those wants . . . Trade is founder and father of enterprise, invention, and exploration.

—*Sir Walter Besant,*
English novelist and historian (1836–1901)

Foreword

Dear Reader,

This book is a great asset and brings detailed and strategic consideration to an area of finance and investment with solid returns and a substantial impact on economic development and growth. In the ever-evolving global business landscape, trade finance stands out as a steadfast pillar – an asset class often overlooked yet brimming with untapped potential in the private markets. I had the privilege of serving as a board member of Canada's export credit agency, EDC. As someone who has navigated the complexities of banking, commodities and trade across continents, I have witnessed firsthand the resilience and strategic value of trade finance. In a world where markets fluctuate and economies face unforeseen challenges, trade finance offers something rare: stability, security and consistent returns.

Trade finance is not a modern invention but a legacy stretching back to the dawn of commerce. Picture this: ancient Mesopotamian traders in 3000 BC laid the groundwork for what we now know as trade finance. Fast-forward to the Roman Empire, the Silk Road and the Italian merchant banks of the 13th century, each era refining and expanding the mechanisms that facilitated global trade and economic growth. By the 18th century, London had become the beating heart of global trade finance, with letters of credit and bankers' acceptances as its pulse. Today, we stand on the brink of a new revolution, where blockchain and AI have entered the scene, bringing efficiency, transparency and speed to the global trade finance process. New opportunities have been created for private investors in trade finance as recent banking regulation reform, including Basel III, has disincentivised banks from using their capital in this space. Nevertheless, it remains profitable and has a reliable recurrence of transactions involving proven counterparties in trade.

Whether you are a seasoned professional, a curious student, or someone new to the financial world, this book opens the door to understanding why trade finance is more relevant than ever. In these pages, you will discover the mechanics of trade finance and its role in mitigating risks, hedging against inflation and seizing opportunities in a volatile global market.

One of the most exciting developments in recent years is the democratisation of trade finance investment. Traditionally, entering this space required significant capital, often limiting access to institutional or professional investors or banks with deep pockets. However, the rise of decentralised finance (DeFi) platforms is changing the game. Now, with as little as $100, investors can participate in trade finance through DeFi's specific investment pools – making this once-exclusive asset class accessible to a broader audience. This shift opens doors for more investors and signals a future where trade finance is both inclusive and innovative.

As you delve into the chapters, you will explore how trade finance has adapted to contemporary challenges, including integrating environmental, social, and governance (ESG) principles, the rise of DeFi, and the unique synergies between small and medium-sized enterprises (SMEs) and global trade houses. Each chapter builds on the last, offering a comprehensive view of an asset class that drives global trade through a strategic avenue for those looking to diversify their portfolios with lower-risk, higher-return investments.

This book is not just a guide but an invitation to view trade finance through a new lens that reveals its potential as a catalyst for sustainable growth and global prosperity. Whether considering trade finance as an investment or simply looking to expand your financial knowledge, you will find valuable insights and actionable strategies within these pages.

In a world where finance can often seem distant and complex, this book offers a refreshing perspective – clear, insightful and directly applicable to the real world. I encourage you to read on, explore the nuances of trade finance, and discover why it stands out as a unique and powerful tool in today's financial landscape.

Sincerely,
Jeffrey Steiner
Chairman & CEO
Canada–Saudi Arabia Business Council

Toronto, Winter 2024
http://ca.linkedin.com/pub/jeffrey-steiner/9/616/146/

Preface

The pages that follow contain snippets from years of trade-finance research. Our wish is to provide the financially interested reader with an insight into trade finance as an investment class.

The first Covid-19 lockdown in spring 2020 put a spanner in the works of the business model for my company Arjan Capital. This forced me to have a fundamental rethink about what our business offered and what a post-pandemic business might look like. Having been exposed daily to trade and payment issues over the years, I began financing short-term trade on a small-scale basis with parties that I knew well.

Arjan Capital assists large-and-mid-cap companies in handling and executing their trade which is mainly aimed towards Central Asia – marginal markets for many – and collecting the outstanding funds. Our USP is to accompany or go on behalf of our client to the country of trade, including places like Kabul or Herat in Afghanistan, where we helped a European leader in its sector win back a lost tender with the Afghan government of that time. We cover a niche that is still of interest to larger companies.

Trade Works

We had observed that the unfinanced trade gap, which we shall discuss later, is enormous. We concluded that trade finance for mid-cap companies is an ample business opportunity even throughout a pandemic.

Research is key. While stocks, bonds, equity trade and foreign exchange have been researched in detail, trade finance has not been well researched and packaged for public consumption. Useful commercial trade information is available from supra-national institutions like the World Bank; the International Monetary Fund (IMF); the International Chamber of Commerce (ICC); and some law and advisory firms.

This was insufficient, so we established our research desk. We decided to create a trade-finance and factoring program discounting good-quality, credit-insured receivables.

Acknowledgements

Research is a fascinating discipline and writing a book is a fascinating experience. I am genuinely grateful for the many brains and voices that have helped me to critically reflect on the truly relevant and stay focused. As a patient reader you are the ultimate judge, and I am grateful hearing your comments or input on the matter.

Much is owed to Grace O'Donnell who helped me get started in the first place. Mohsin Naveed continues spending uncountable hours on research and providing his own valuable input. We count ourselves lucky to have met Judith Engst in Germany, who not only edited the German version of this book, but as a bilingual financial journalist provided the critical thoughts required in reviewing this new edition. My sincere thanks go as well to Daniel Haddad whose in-depth knowledge of law and trade kept us safe.

The process of writing a book is like having a secret that you are desperate to share but know you should not. Eventually, you need the generous reader willing to plough their way through what still feels like a building site of words and sentences. Thank you to my friends and family members for generously accepting my request to read through ever-changing drafts and for providing valuable feedback.

Without the love and encouragement of my wife Ashoob and my family, I might still be sitting in the garden chewing on a virtual pen. My most enormous thank you goes to you.

Andreas Schweitzer
Spring 2025
office@arjancapital.com

Summary

Trade finance, often overlooked by many investors, is akin to a 'Snow White' in the world of asset allocation – a hidden beauty waiting to be awakened. The COVID-19 pandemic exposed the vast, unfinanced trade gap, drawing the attention of sophisticated investors seeking stable, low-volatility returns uncorrelated with traditional capital markets.

My purpose in writing this book is to provide you, the reader, with valuable insights into the possible opportunities offered by trade finance, whether you are a prudent private investor or a corporate investor looking to capitalise on a credit-insured market of significant scale.

In this second edition, I have included my contributions to the *Forbes* Finance Council. I've been a member of the Council since 2023 and have published a series of articles about trade finance. These articles cover the transformative role of decentralised finance (DeFi), the importance of accurate benchmarking and the rising influence of environmental, social and governance (ESG)-driven investments. These insights offer unique perspectives rarely found elsewhere, providing you with cutting-edge knowledge to navigate the evolving trade finance landscape.

Trade Works

Throughout this book, you'll discover why trade finance is becoming an increasingly attractive investment option:

1. Traditional financial institutions retreat from this market, creating opportunities for private investment firms to step in.
2. The trade finance gap, estimated by the World Economic Forum at $2.5 to $6 trillion, presents a significant investment opportunity.
3. Due to comprehensive risk mitigation strategies, trade finance lending carries a lower risk than general corporate lending.
4. Historically, trade finance has been instrumental in the global success of companies like Mitsubishi and Walmart.
5. Trade finance provides stable revenues, even in times of economic uncertainty, supported by credit insurance.
6. Long-term investment relationships in trade finance offer predictable returns and excellent stability.
7. Following successful investors like Warren Buffett, more are turning to secured trade finance as a strategic investment.
8. Trade finance can deliver predictable returns without needing to 'beat the market', making it a valuable option during economic downturns.

9. The global economy relies heavily on trade. When aligned with the UN's sustainable development goals, trade finance can create a substantial positive impact while offering profitability – an asset class that serves both financial and societal good.

As you conclude this book, you may find yourself inspired to explore trade finance as an investment avenue, adopting the mindset of 'invest well, sleep well'. You may also determine that this asset class doesn't align with your strategy. Either way, I invite you to reach out – whether to discuss potential investment opportunities, explore new insights or exchange thoughts.

You can contact us at office@artistradeinvest.com or +44 7881 782 041 (also available on WhatsApp, Telegram, Signal and Threema). For more resources and insights, visit our website at www.artistradeinvest.com. We look forward to hearing from you and continuing the conversation.

Introduction

I t is a curious paradox: while the stock markets command persistent attention in the media, with every fluctuation in share prices, corporate actions, central bank decisions and market reactions dissected in minute detail, the financial mechanisms that drive global trade remain largely disregarded. Despite facilitating a staggering $24 trillion in annual commerce, trade finance only garners a fraction of the media spotlight. It represents only one-eighth of the stock market's turnover and is perceived as a niche field demanding significant expertise to navigate profitably, addressing the needs of corporate or professional investors only and not suited for retail investors.

Trade finance is not only an essential engine of international commerce. It offers compelling opportunities for professional investors, often with less complexity than one might assume. My aim in the following chapters is to bring greater visibility to this dynamic sector and ensure it receives the coverage it deserves. Before delving into the specifics, I would like to share how I discovered this fascinating field and why I believe it holds great promise for anyone interested in economics and investment.

How I got into trade finance

I always knew that I would work in the world of business but never expected that much of my career would revolve around trade and financing. However, 40 years later, I cannot imagine doing anything else.

My grandfather and father ran a terry-cloth fashion business in Tübingen, in Swabia, southern Germany, which started in 1924. It covered the whole value chain. The company did not only weave or dye. My grandfather bought the cotton, spun it, then bleached, coloured and wove it. After that, the fashion department designed clothes made from terry cloth. When I was 20 years old, my father allowed me to train for a summer in his firm, which sparked my interest in trade. I found the textile industry fascinating and glamorous.

My general trade knowledge from school was far from adequate to provide me with an understanding of the textile industry. I would have had to spend a few more years learning about yarns, threads, shuttles and dyeing and understanding how the business operated. I was truly happy to finally be out of education and wanted to apply the trade knowledge I had just obtained from my degree at the École Supérieure de Commerce in Neuchâtel in French-speaking Switzerland. I was restless and looking forward to being out in the world. More studying was not on the agenda.

I completed my Swiss military service as a *Luftbeobachter*, an 'air observer', supporting mobile anti-aircraft radar stations in the Swiss valleys, from remote locations in the surrounding mountains. Our training included mountain climbing, both on foot and skis. Regrettably, our division soon became a victim of fast-moving technology, but I have truly great memories from my sporty Swiss army days. In 1981 A. Sarasin & Cie, the prestigious Swiss private bank based in Basel, took me on as their very first trainee.

A year after joining, I was lucky enough to be offered a junior position at the newly opened Sarasin office in St Andrew's Hill, next to St Paul's Cathedral in London. Inhaling the air of business in the City of London motivated me to expand my knowledge again. I studied portfolio management at the London School of Economics while working as a trainee at the bank during the day. But two years later, I left banking; it just did not inspire me. To make matters worse, I had no idea what truly did inspire me.

One winter evening in our family chalet in Fidaz, a picturesque hamlet above Flims in the Swiss Grisons mountains, my dear school friend and music lover, Urs (a quite unique Swiss name), and I decided to add a language to our repertoire, but which one? I considered Portuguese; Urs opted for Italian, the language of music. With the memory of car-free Sundays during the oil crisis of the seventies still fresh in my mind, I thought Arabic might be a more useful language for me to study.

There was also a family connection to Arabic. My grandfather, Hermann, bought much of his long-staple cotton in Egypt and was a fluent Arabic speaker, as was my aunt, Professor Ursula Schweitzer, who created and chaired the Department of Egyptology at the University of Basel. But in the end, Urs and I chose to study Spanish. One January morning in 1984, we put the car on the train and arrived one day later in sunny Malaga. We mastered a reasonable command of Spanish, before realising later that year that it was time to get serious about life. And so we left Malaga and its Flamenco nights to look for a job, but it was easier said than done.

Every 24-year-old is allowed to have some optimistic expectations, at least for a while, but reality should sink in eventually. Later that year, and after a few months of job interviews that led nowhere, I was lucky again.

I applied for a job as an assistant treasurer; the recruiter encouraged me to meet her client, whom she described as an out-of-the-ordinary chocolate company. Jacobs Suchard (today part of Kraft Foods International Inc.) was extraordinary, a multibillion-Swiss-francs food company that had recently merged with Suchard Chocolate and moved its headquarters from Bremen in the north of Germany to the shores of Lake Zurich.

The mid-eighties were the days of Apple, Microsoft PCs and IBM ATs as well as Lotus 1-2-3, an early spreadsheet program. Just before then, Jacobs Suchard had suffered an inexplicable loss of tens of millions of Swiss francs. The reason for this financial depression was eventually identified: the sudden increase in the price of green coffee beans could not be passed on to the German hausfrau, probably the most important customer demographic for Jacobs Coffee at the time.

The Jacobs Suchard management was now constantly alert about identifying and managing commodity and currency risks. I was placed in a team charged with developing a PC/ spreadsheet-based risk-monitoring tool. Over the next year, I implemented this software across the Jacobs Suchard operating companies in Europe and in North and South America, accumulating a fair share of know-how about trade risk.

One Friday afternoon in June 1986, my boss, the chief controller who knew of my desire to work abroad, peeked into my small Zurich lake-view office. His message was brief but exciting:

'We need someone in Panama for a new role. Would you be interested in moving abroad for a few years?' The position would be hosted within Banco Aleman-Panameño, Jacobs Suchard's trade-finance bank. 'No rush,' he said. 'Let me know by Monday morning.'

Three weeks later, I was working and living in Panama City, in the only country in Central America where the Atlantic is in the north and the Pacific in the south.

Working in the trade and finance department of a food multinational was a world away from Swiss private banking and the London Eurobond boom, my only real market experiences up to then. In Panama, I administered the commodity-sales operations of the group's entire Americas operations. As a 26-year-old, I was responsible for about half-a-billion Swiss francs.

Structuring and financing trade was the nucleus of all business in my mind. I could not have found a better opportunity for on-the-ground and fast-track learning about trade and its financing. Apart from British and Dutch Guiana, I visited every country that had coffee or cocoa plantations or a Jacobs Suchard production plant, from San Salvador and Guatemala in the north, to Brazil and Argentina in the south of the continent.

In Panama, I continued to work in the trade-finance industry at the Crédit Français International, the French trade-finance bank of the group. I left Jacobs Suchard in 1990.

In each new country that I worked in, I learned the local basics. With the help of the group's finance expert, I learned how to manage a highly inflationary currency with its explosive interest rates. I became an expert in commodity trade deals by learning about documentary credit, risk identification, evaluation and mitigation, shipping and collection of money. I worked within the harshest trade environment at the time (i.e. Argentina) to the least harsh (i.e. Panama and Switzerland).

During my years in the industry, more change happened in finance than in trade. The speed of transactions and the precision of technology has changed the execution in the trade-financing industry, but not the fundamentals of assessing a trade. The invention of blockchain has meant that trade transactions which were previously heavily documented are now executed more efficiently, more transparently and are less costly. Overall, trade finance has become more secure.

Back to lockdown. As a result of opportunity rather than by strategy, I started to put my money into trades where I knew enough about at least one of the parties and enough of the details. The number of trades grew organically into a business — the Artis Trade Invest model. Artis is managed by the same team as our other FCA-regulated company, Arjan Capital. Artis enables investors to safely ride the wave of the rapidly growing trade-finance gap by investing in this low-risk asset class, which produces stable returns and helps to balance world trade. During the times of negative or low interest rates I used — and still use — our credit-insured trade finance concept as a short-term cash management tool.

Artis's trade business today

At Artis, our business space is simple: we see an opportunity where banks don't finance SME trade. Now our main focus is on business within Europe, particularly on the Iberian Peninsula. However, we are also open to new trade finance opportunities, as you will see later in this book.

We re-entered the world of trade in 2009, mainly in Central Asia, a market we had little knowledge of.

Due to the geopolitical development during the following ten years, we decided to re-evaluate our business strategy and geographical operation space. The more we researched, the more we realised that there are ample trade opportunities at our European business doorstep, in the UK, some European countries, Spain or even Switzerland. Over time I reflected on what I had learned, and the result was our current Artis Trade Invest niche business model focusing on trading pharma and fuel within the Iberian Peninsula, both of which are regulated markets and under EU law. A fertile ground for a rewarding niche business. Why do such niche markets exist and why is everyone not rushing for the opportunity?

Small markets as an attractive niche

Despite the attractive financial rewards in percentage terms, some markets are often too small in monetary terms and complex in compliance for large-scale finance institutions to be interested in or capable of deploying their costly resources. It is not only the yield that counts but the overall revenue in pounds or euros that can be generated in such a market. The current pharma and fuel niche markets we trade in are measured in the tens, not hundreds, of millions in turnover, therefore they are attractive for specialised trade firms like ourselves. In other words, we satisfy ourselves with giant trade cake's (large) financial crumbs.

We constantly monitor other parts of the world for trade opportunities, particularly Africa, Latin America and Saudi Arabia (see Chapter 9: Artis's Growing Business Space: Exploring Trade in Saudi Arabia'). Still, as long as we encounter trade opportunities in regulated European markets with healthy returns, we see no argument for seeking more risk for our and our lenders' monies. In Europe, we understand the environment. The travel time is shorter, we know the legal system and, by and large, we cover a few Western European languages as a team. There are quite a few arguments to remain focused on good old Europe, although for reasons of diversification alone it can also make sense to have a small foothold in other countries and regions.

Further research showed that the pharmaceutical and medical market, mainly spot trades, require credit terms to credit-insured buyers. The term 'spot trade' refers to the purchase and sale of goods or commodities for immediate delivery and payment, often at the prevailing market price. It is commonly used for transactions requiring swift execution. At the time of writing, we finance pharmaceutical and medical trades on the Iberian Peninsula, i.e., Spain and Portugal. In addition, there is now funding for diesel deliveries from the wholesaler in Spain to the petrol station in Spain, all yielding between 12–18 per cent per annum.

Too good to be true? Not too good to last? Possibly, but then we will get our funds back in 35 to 90 days and deploy them to other market niches.

Niches due to ambitious ESG requirements

Other background factors to consider are the so-called ESG (environmental, social and governance) reasons for why dirty products are not financed. The fuel can be sold and burned in the car, but a financial institution cannot have it on the balance sheet due to ESG requirements. If there is no ESG-compliant substitute for such goods, trading in the goods is still required, and a financier is still necessary. Another example is that some financial institutions do not finance chocolate stock or production. What is suddenly wrong with the Easter Bunny or Father Christmas? The sugar. Sugar kills. The law now limits sugar consumption, but financing is out of the question. Fast-moving fashion is being accused, and probably quite rightly, of being harmful to the environment, let alone the discussion about labour conditions in South-East Asia. However, people are still wearing clothes, driving diesel and petrol cars, smoking cigarettes and consuming sugar products. A discrepancy between regulation and reality remains. Is it therefore reprehensible to do business with it? I leave this to the interpretation of my esteemed readers.

Why investors should pay more attention to trade finance or '*la nature a horreur du vide*'

The trade finance landscape is undergoing a significant transformation, presenting a timely opportunity for investors. Banks have been the dominant players in this sector for decades, providing crucial short-term funding to small- and medium-sized enterprises (SMEs) engaged in international trade.

However, stringent regulatory requirements have increasingly curtailed their involvement. Prohibitive compliance costs and low profitability are driving financial institutions away.

This withdrawal of traditional lenders and in particular banks has created a compelling market opportunity. Nature abhors a vacuum. Unencumbered by the onerous regulatory burdens banks face, private debt firms are stepping in to fill this void. My company is one example, operating within a well-defined and controlled legal and regulatory framework but free from the excessive bureaucracy that has stymied banks. Trade finance, though often overlooked, offers an attractive, highly profitable business model – at least this is how we see and deal with it. When executed with diligence, the risks are remarkably low and the returns are stable. The sector's lack of correlation with the stock market further enhances its appeal to invest, seeking diversification in turbulent times.

To my knowledge, trade finance has never sparked a financial crisis, yet trade-finance supply – money – has always been affected by a financial crisis. The trade sector (especially its SMEs) is an integral part of the UN sustainable development goals (SDGs). The regrowth in supply contributes to a healthier economy. Trade has always proved to be the catalyst for economic growth. Historically, trade finance has had the lowest default rates, regardless of financial crises.

The aim of this book is to guide the reader through the historical success of trade financing used by companies such as Mitsubishi and Walmart to grow into the billion-dollar powerhouses they are today. Investors' minds will understand the distinctive financing options for trade available and the rigorous due diligence required for crafting a financing arrangement.

It is my wish that at the end of this book, you will have a working knowledge of the trade-financing process. You will comprehend how to best leverage and include this trade investment opportunity within your own investment strategy, to balance your portfolio in the face of an uncertain financial market and evolving global economic crisis.

Chapter 1:

The Purpose and Impact of Trade Finance and its Suitability as an Investment

Trade finance is the lifeblood of global commerce. It ensures businesses can operate seamlessly across borders by providing the necessary capital to bridge the time gap between production and payment.

The existence of this time gap is a result of the differing needs of exporters and importers. Exporters' interest in seeking immediate payment for goods to maintain liquidity, are diametrically opposed to importers' interest, who, also motivated by the same liquidity concerns, seek deferred payment terms. These terms can range from 30 to 120 days, allowing them to pay suppliers once they have sold the goods. To reconcile these opposing needs, a financier steps in, bridging this gap, providing the necessary liquidity to facilitate the required payment terms and with it the transaction itself.

Access to trade finance has become vital not only in developed markets but also in emerging economies. By underpinning international trade, trade finance catalyses economic development and a compelling investment opportunity, offering stability and potential for profit with relatively low risk.

Two examples of what a trade financier/investor does

Money is the lubricant in the machinery of international trade. It ensures that this engine runs smoothly – and is most needed where the trade transaction might otherwise come to a squeaking halt.

Case 1: Buying building materials for DIY projects

A European client contacted Artis to request funding for its construction and lighting business. The company needed to stock its store with locally based goods and raw building materials for families preferring DIY for their home projects.

The client was looking to accumulate a variety of goods from different sellers all over the country to put these packages together. We investigated the company and its business partners to find that the business model, although new, was well received in the small but affluent local town.

We purchased the imports for the buyer with an open account and put the tenor, i.e. the duration of the contracts, at 30 to 60 days. If our client paid the amount owed to Artis in the first 30 days, they would benefit from a small discount on the total amount due. The importer met the 30-day tenor and asked us to reinvest.

As a result, our investment had a gross return of 11 per cent at the end of a year, while at the same time the borrower saved close to 25 per cent on their annual purchase cost by continuously paying ahead of the agreed tenor date. Prepayment does not reduce revenues as it allows us to reinvest earlier. Both parties win and develop a long-standing business relationship that continues to provide positive gains.

Case 2: The Omani miller and corn trader

In many countries outside Asia, corn accounts for a very high percentage of daily food intake. While corn used to just feed humans and animals, it is now used to produce ethanol, an important ingredient in gasoline production and so also now feeds car engines as well.

Although corn isn't as glamorous as, say, diamonds, it is a highly sought-after product. Our Omani miller had to pay for the corn upon transfer of documents when the merchandise was loaded onto the ship at a port on the Caspian Sea. The miller had a cashflow shortage until the corn was paid for by the final buyer. He used some of the corn in his own mill to produce bakery products. Artis facilitated a purchase-and-sales agreement.

We had to analyse the trader and the importer, as well as the business history and payment history of the importer. We decided to take on the purchase and sale transaction. Once the agreement was signed, Artis financed a vessel full of corn – about 3,000 metric tons – with a tenor of 45 days. This has become a repeat business and works as smoothly as a Swiss clock.

Trade agreements go smoothly when the necessary leg-work has been done at the outset. If a trade transaction runs into issues it is often due to a lack of insufficient analysis or documentation.

Dieu est dans les détails (God is in the details), as the French say rather than the proverbial devil that the German language refers to in the same situation.

So far, we have never had to absorb a loss. Investment returns range from an annualised 8 per cent to a rare 36 per cent per annum, averaging out at around 10 per cent per annum net to the investors. Much depends on the type of investment, the structure and the jurisdictions involved.

Is it a purchase-and-sale agreement with entitlement to a profit margin share or a case of pure financing with a margin? The best deal sometimes is the deal not done. We consciously decline many transactions. Of course, we are in business to do trade deals, not to turn them down, but a critical mind is crucial. Our reinvestment rate is above 95 per cent. When an SME successfully closes out a contract or a financing agreement is scheduled to end, we redeploy the funds immediately, often by extending the current facility or by adjusting the funding to the client's new needs.

A high rate of reinvestment ensures that funds are not sitting in the bank account producing at worse negative yields, hence costing revenue. Reinvestment gives confidence to buyers and sellers to successfully grow their businesses, together with a positive impact on the world of trade. The high reinvestment rates make trade business sustainable and offer continued room for portfolio growth. Artis has become our hub for profitable trade-finance investments.

If a transaction gets delayed and the tenor date cannot be met, discussions are held immediately with the debtor. In most cases the delay is a matter of days, not even weeks. Of the 0.02 per cent default rate in trade finance, 77 per cent of those accounts were rectified with payment extension. Trade firms can roll over accounts more easily and with less administrative burden than institutional structures like banks.

Should a borrower show signs of default or if signs of fraud become a sudden concern during the execution of a trade, we immediately notify the credit insurer who takes over the management of the case. Where a trade is not insured, the lender must jump into action on its own or its investor's behalf. In such an uninsured case, it is good to have additional collateral in place. While such collateral might serve as leverage for renegotiation, it should always cover the outstanding amounts plus accumulated recovery costs. There is an obvious reason why we stick to credit-insured trades.

It's all about building resilient global supply chains

Trade finance is essential in building and maintaining supply chains, ensuring companies' operational flow and growth even during economic disruptions.

Supply chain resilience is vital. It is not only about keeping goods moving; it's about ensuring that businesses have the liquidity and security needed to respond well to challenges and reduce the risk of disruptions. Remember the financial crisis of 2008 when trade finance played a pivotal role in stabilising supply chains, helping businesses to continue operating? Trade finance is indispensable when supply chain disruptions pose significant risks to global trade and financial stability.

Trade finance: A catalyst of global growth and sustainability

As the global economy evolves, trade finance will play an increasingly important role in driving growth, sustainability and social impact. By unlocking the potential of emerging markets, building resilient supply chains and integrating ESG principles into investment decisions, trade finance is helping to shape the future of global commerce.

Trade finance offers investors the possibility of achieving financial and social returns. By understanding and leveraging the power of trade finance, they can contribute to global development while potentially seeing attractive and stable returns in a volatile market. In this way, trade finance is not just a financial tool but a catalyst for positive change in the world.

The demand for trade financing is still growing and the opportunities for generating profits in this sector look compelling. Why are import and export companies, small and medium-sized enterprises (SMEs), struggling to find suitable financing today?

I briefly addressed the matter in the introduction. Let us look together at the factors that have led to this situation in more detail now.

Challenges: Why banks are currently withdrawing from trade financing

The term 'trade finance gap' gained prominence after the 2008 financial crisis. This period introduced a new era of trade-related sanctions, tighter regulations (such as Basel III and IV), stricter lending policies and the rise of fintech, artificial intelligence (AI) and big data. Basel regulations are international banking rules designed to ensure financial stability by requiring banks to hold enough capital to cover risks. Basel III and IV focus on strengthening bank resilience, managing credit risks and maintaining liquidity, especially in times of financial stress. Steeply increased regulatory requirements have made trade finance more capital-intensive for banks, regardless of its relative risk sector. While banks may find higher profitability in areas such as retail banking, at least large-cap trade finance still plays a crucial role in their portfolios.

In summary, these shifts have led financial institutions to reconsider and often reduce their trade lending offers, particularly for SMEs, thus bringing the trade finance gap into sharper focus. This has been exacerbated by a reduction in correspondent banking relationships (CBRs), as globally active banks have retrenched from riskier developing markets due to increased regulatory scrutiny and lower profit margins.

The rejection rate for SME credit applications by banks remains above 50 per cent globally and continues to rise. The primary driver of this trend is the tightening regulatory environment. As John Denton, Secretary General of the International Chamber of Commerce (ICC), said in a letter to the *Financial Times* ahead of the G20 Summit 2020, the associated costs of transactions are now stifling trade and potentially threatening supply chains.

With regulatory oversight only expected to intensify, the trade finance gap is unlikely to narrow in the foreseeable future. In fact, future financial crises or disruptions, such as the COVID-19 pandemic, may widen the gap even further.

Trade houses support small and medium-sized enterprises: The synergies for international trade

International trade presents significant opportunities for SMEs but comes with challenges. As described, a significant hurdle is securing the necessary financing now that banks no longer offer it.

Enterprises must find reliable partners abroad and safeguard their trades against risks. By acting as intermediaries or facilitating the exchange of goods between suppliers and buyers across countries, modern trade houses are increasingly stepping in.

As times have evolved, the services offered by trade houses have broadened to include financing, risk mitigation, quality control and compliance to make international markets even more accessible to SMEs.

Understanding the challenges for SMEs in international trade

In international trade, SMEs encounter challenges that vary depending on their business nature and target markets.

One significant hurdle is access to finance. SMEs often need help securing international trade finance, due to limited credit histories in foreign markets and a lack of substantial assets or collateral, making it challenging to meet traditional banking requirements.

Another quest is finding reliable partners. Identifying trustworthy suppliers, distributors and agents in foreign markets can be daunting. There are risks such as fraud, non-payment, delivery of substandard products and last-minute withdrawal by buyers.

SMEs frequently grapple with regulatory and compliance issues. Navigating the varying trade laws, customs requirements and product standards across different countries is complex. It can lead to costly delays and additional expenses.

- **Language and cultural barriers:** Effective communication is crucial despite the democratisation of the English language. Language differences and cultural misunderstandings can complicate negotiations, contract drafting and relationship-building.
- **Logistics and shipping issues:** Delays, substandard quality or inaccurate quantity of goods can disrupt supply chains and damage customer relationships.

Moreover, political and economic instability in foreign markets poses additional risks. For example, geopolitical events have caused global supply chain disruptions, leaving SMEs vulnerable to blocked market access and increased competition, leading to price drops and higher production costs due to rising energy and fertiliser prices. Businesses in sanctioned countries need help securing conventional financing, let alone the cost aspect of financing.

The above highlights the complexity of international trade for SMEs and the need for careful planning and strategic decision-making to navigate these obstacles successfully.

Safety mechanisms offered by trade houses

Trade houses can provide a suite of safety mechanisms leveraging their expertise and extensive networks in international markets, helping SMEs broaden their global footprint.

One key mechanism is factoring, where trade houses buy a business's accounts receivable at a discounted rate, offering immediate cash for future buyer payments (see Chapter 3: 'How Trade Finance Works: Methods, Means and Tools'). This approach is particularly beneficial for SMEs, as it bypasses the need for asset collateral or extensive credit checks required by banks, thus not affecting the company's balance sheet and creditworthiness.

Unlike banks, many trade houses provide financing by collateralising the goods traded rather than relying on the company's balance sheets. This helps ensure that SMEs in their early stages of development, where they may not have substantial assets or a solid financial track record, still get access to growth opportunities.

Trade houses conduct comprehensive due diligence and risk assessments, evaluating the creditworthiness of both sellers and their international partners to mitigate the risks of non-payment and trade disputes.

Trade houses can enable SMEs' compliance with foreign market laws and regulations, potentially reducing legal disputes. To further enhance transaction security, trade houses often collateralise the goods being traded and require fixed down payments from buyers.

Moreover, their global networks can be beneficial. Suppose a buyer withdraws at the last minute. In that case, trade houses can find an alternative, safeguarding SMEs from sudden disruptions and financial losses.

Trade houses are helpful allies in supporting SMEs in the complex world of international trade. However, selecting the right trade house requires thorough research.

Factors to consider when selecting a trade house

The choice of a trade house can significantly impact the success and security of cross-border transactions. Some factors businesses should consider when making an informed selection:

- **Industry expertise:** A trade house with experience and expertise in the industry or sector relevant to the business can provide valuable insights and customised solutions.
- **Global presence:** A reputable trade house should have a vast global network of trusted traders, buyers and sellers and a presence in key geographic regions critical to the business's international expansion.
- **Financial stability and resources:** The financial stability of the trade house is essential. SMEs should assess whether the

trade house has the necessary resources to support their trade activities, including financing options and risk-management capabilities.

- **Cultural and language proficiency:** A trade house proficient in the target markets' languages and cultures can bridge potential communication gaps and facilitate smoother transactions.
- **Reputation and track record:** SMEs should research the trade house's history, client testimonials and trade cases to ensure reliability and trustworthiness.

According to World Bank data, SMEs account for over 90 per cent of businesses and more than 50 per cent of employment worldwide. Yet their participation in international trade is limited. Nurturing these SMEs to thrive in international markets can play a role in changing the status quo.

Working with trade houses can be one of the solutions to help SMEs grow and expand their business in unknown markets. Supporting SMEs can help limit risks, contributing to a more robust economy and global trade stability.

In nurturing the potential of SMEs, we invest in a brighter, more equitable future for both businesses and societies across the globe.

Investing in trade finance: Profits in line with social responsibility

Trade finance, the linchpin of international trade, empowers businesses worldwide to engage in transactions with assurance. It encompasses a collection of financial instruments that facilitate the exchange of goods and services across borders, mitigating risks like non- or delayed payment while ensuring smoother commercial flows and bolstering the global economy. Key components such as letters of credit, export credit and insurance provide transactional security and improve liquidity by offering financing against receivables or goods pending shipment or payment.

Despite this critical importance, the global trade finance gap, estimated at $2.6 trillion in 2025, remains a barrier to growth. This gap especially hurts SMEs across sectors as they struggle to secure the financing they need to innovate and expand. In advanced economies, 60–80 per cent of local businesses can access trade finance facilities. In some regions such as West Africa, only 25 per cent of trade benefits from trade finance support and at significantly higher financing costs.

Trade finance facilitates the bond between financial returns and social responsibility. By providing an opportunity for stable and attractive returns, it offers investors a compelling alternative to traditional asset classes. Simultaneously, its focus on supporting sustainable and inclusive development aligns returns with broader social and environmental goals.

Entire regions like West Africa, with swelling trade finance coverage could increase annual trade flows promoting socially inclusive global trade networks. Organisations such as the International Finance Corporation are already addressing these gaps by providing supply chain finance and supporting essential trade flows, which could serve as a model for other financial institutions.

Non-banking, or in other words private debt companies, can play an important and profitable role in closing the funding gap. This is what we do at Artis Trade Invest. We manage the opportunity to invest in trade finance and are convinced that high profits are possible at low risk. Of course, we all know too well that past performance is no guarantee for future returns.

Chapter 2:

The Evolution of Trade Finance:
A Bit of History

Since the nineteenth century, the financial world has witnessed many crises and events of lesser magnitude that have changed how the financial ecosystem works.

This chapter highlights and discusses some of the significant past events, their implications for trade finance and how this asset class built the foundation for the fortunes of many financial institutions.

The British merchant banks

The 'Central European Panic' was the name given to the declining state of European banking in the spring of 1931. The summer that followed was marked by significant difficulties for banks throughout Central Europe. First, banks in Austria declared insolvency, promptly followed by those in Hungary and Germany. Central to the crisis were the London merchant banks.

Before the panic began, a credit boom spread throughout Central Europe. Banks with dwindling amounts of capital were guaranteeing the bills of sale of foreign merchants. Funding European merchants did not require any extra financial resources and allowed the banks to earn considerable returns on their investments.

Capital issues began arising across the globe a few months into 1931 when the Great Depression swept through Central Europe. As currencies depreciated, local governments introduced more capital controls on banking institutions. The action was meant to reduce fallouts associated with the banking panic; in truth, it only pushed local economies deeper into depression. These controls were known as the standstill agreements.

The balance sheets of several British merchant banks suggest that the banks' exposure to Central Europe debt accounted for a mere 6 per cent of their direct portfolio holdings. However, the banks were additionally exposed through the bankers' acceptance (BA), an offer almost exclusive to merchant banks.

This financial instrument was a specific type of bill of exchange used by international merchants to finance their trade activities. The principle was simple: a bank in London guaranteed a company's debt by accepting a commission in exchange.

For example, if a Colombian exporter sold goods to a German importer, they would normally be paid between 30 and 90 days later. Most exporters were paid upon receipt of the goods by the buyer. If the exporter wanted to be paid prior to the goods' arrival, the seller could opt to draw a bill of exchange on the importer (the debtor), ordering the buyer to pay the bill holder the amount of the transaction at an agreed-upon date in the future. The merchant would then try to discount the bill on the London market.

In May 1931, the largest Austrian bank, Creditanstalt, declared insolvency, triggering a regional banking collapse in the two months that followed. With newly implemented bans, all payments abroad were frozen and Central European banks were forced to create arrangements with their foreign creditors to settle the payments of their debts.

Lenders in London would not have paid a discounted bill from a foreign merchant without a guarantee of some kind that they would receive payment from the importer. The BA solved this problem as it allowed the exporter to draw the bill on the accepting London bank with whom the importer/ debtor had an arrangement rather than directly on the importer/debtor.

To be accepted by a merchant bank, an exporter was required to prove that they had shipped the goods to the importer and that the importer would pay the balance soon. Upon successful examination of the evidence, the bank accepted the bill. They stamped the bill with their emblem for a fee.

With the signature of a reputable London house on it, the bill was turned into a saleable security which could easily be discounted on the London market by the seller at the prevailing interest rate. By doing this, the bank committed to pay the bill at maturity regardless of whether payment had been remitted by the importer/debtor. Acceptance was an attractive line of business for British merchant banks and in the nineteenth century the merchant bankers had a near-monopoly on the acceptance business.

During the Great Depression brought on by the First World War, merchant banks faced the difficulty of the standstill agreements. The limitations imposed by the Federal Reserve meant that the struggling countries of Austria, Hungary and Germany could not convert their local currencies into sterling to pay the debts owed to British banks. Even a flourishing bank could not transfer funds to the UK unless they had claims in foreign currency.

The standstill and liquidity freezes resulted in months of missed payments that greatly contributed to the downfall of the British merchant banks. Even though bills could not be paid due to the standstill, federal legislation did not include any relief provisions for banks who were still legally responsible for paying for goods at their agreed maturity date.

With all their assets tied up, British merchant banks had no choice but to liquidate their assets to meet their committed financial obligations. To recover from these losses, they were advised by the Bank of England to continue restricting credit. Thus, the banks hit hardest by losses were not the least capitalised but the most exposed to Central European acceptances.

The Bank of England considered merchant banks to be crucial in preserving the position of the London market. As a result, it bailed out 20 of the 22 merchant banks struggling as a by-product of the standstill agreement. Through this intervention, most were able to stay in business.

The Bank of England knew that acceptances were never going to go away entirely and decided to reopen the London market. Instead of requiring only minimal information from exporters looking to sell their discounted bills, the Bank began to integrate a careful peer-review business analysis before providing international and domestic acceptances to unverified merchants. This allowed for a massive step forward in bank recovery and resulted in a new industry standard.

The Kuwaiti market crash

The Souk Al-Manakh, better known as the Kuwaiti stock-market crash of 1982, is a prime example of trade financing remaining solid in the face of a local economic downturn.

At its peak, its market capitalisation was the third highest in the world, behind the United States and Japan, but shares were purchased using post-dated cheques. This created a completely unregulated expansion of credit in Kuwait that inevitably came to a grinding halt when post-dated cheques were not honoured, creating an unprecedented chain reaction of cheques bouncing like balloons. These bounced cheques, from 6,000 different investors, reached nearly US$94 billion (the equivalent of US$260.5 billion in 2021).

A recession began on a national scale that disrupted investments and impacted stocks across the country. All the banks in Kuwait collapsed except for one – held up by trade financing and the central bank. The crash set off a recession that rippled through the global markets. The National Bank of Kuwait worked with importers and exporters to finance trade throughout the region, which had yet to be repaid.

With a small bailout from the government, the bank was able to keep its doors open with each delayed payment that it received, immediately reinvesting it back into financing more trade.

We see this same trend in any market we investigate; even during crashing stock markets and global economic depression, trade financing has always remained a source of investing and profitability. One of the reasons it has remained such a constant is because trade itself is a constant. Most industries are working across the global markets, which means the international transport of goods and services. Trade financing has withstood the test of time, war and economic depression.

Before the GFC, trade financing used to rely mainly on bank financing. During the post-financial-crisis era, due to strict regulations, banks started to back off from providing this support, especially to SMEs, which opened the door for alternative financing opportunities to fill the trade-finance gap.

The first record of an entity other than a bank facilitating a trade-finance arrangement points to the sōgō shōshas in Japan. These general-trading firms exemplify the longevity and sturdiness of trade finance. They not only withstood multiple market crashes and global regulation setbacks, but they have been able to grow into a global powerhouse today.

The sōgō shōshas of Japan

Sōgō shōsha is the name of a group of several trading companies that the Japanese organised to meet their internal needs for business capital. A group of wealthy Japanese businessmen created a small, single entity that served to finance emerging businesses, to propel them into the global market.

What started as a single entity quickly decentralised after the Second World War, when the sōgō shōshas switched their lending model to acquire 10 different companies by 1955.

The sōgō shōsha framework was formalised in 1960, at the start of the Japanese post-war economic boom. With trade moving from strictly regulated to the free market, Japan focused on low-technology and non-differentiated exports to increase trade volume. It also diversified the products it marketed internationally, from vending-machine snacks to the automobile industry.

Japan was a developing economy growing fast after opening its ports to foreign vessels and encouraging new industry. As Japanese trading evolved in the 1970s and '80s, traders refined their processes. They managed business during a time of war, enhanced their risk-management systems, strengthened their corporate governance and started taking inventory of their unprofitable assets. As time went on, private trade was gradually permitted and accelerated the free trade market as the sōgō shōshas were being formed.

The sōgō shōshas are the organisers for various industries, providing products and market development. They act as Japan's wholesalers/suppliers and optimise the supply chains of the Japanese industry, helping to provide capital for the raw material, energy and technology needs of Japanese SMEs while aiding businesses to coordinate the manufacturing and retail sectors.

Simultaneously, they market the products of Japanese companies overseas. Using this operational system, the economy and businesses skyrocketed.

The sōgō shōshas act as corporate middlemen or as a special niche of trade financers. They do not own the resources or have the means to mass-produce products, yet they have maintained their Fortune 500 status since 1996. In this model, there are two ways the firm could increase its earnings. One is to handle goods they trade on a larger scale, meaning millions of tons of coal, grain, paper or pulp or hundreds of thousands of computers.

The other way to increase profits is to apply their trading expertise to other items, including higher-value items such as motor vehicles, aeroplanes and medical equipment. This is what is called a scope, increasing the kinds of goods they trade. A single sōgō shōsha handles around 30,000 different products on average – everything from noodles to aeroplanes or from chopsticks to satellites as the saying goes. The handling of such a wide variety of items in such huge volumes is a unique characteristic of the sōgō shōsha and has allowed them to flourish despite economic challenges.

When the 2008 GFC hit, the sōgō shōshas seemed unfazed. Shoei Utsuda, the president of Mitsui, believed the sōgō shōshas were safe in the economic downturn. In *The Economist* of December 2008, he said: 'We have diversity in our industries and our geographies, so we are protected.' And he was undeniably correct. The sōgō shōshas were able to navigate their way out of the turmoil of the surrounding financial landscape by increasing their trade investments and continuing to market their products internationally.

In 2021 there were seven sōgō shōshas in Japan, including Mitsubishi, a name known worldwide. The average sales volume of one of the big five sōgō shōshas is about $123 billion, net profits exceed $3 billion and assets average around $80 billion per company.

Mitsubishi, known most widely as a car manufacturer, also owns the processed and distributed food that it sells in convenience stores in which it holds a stake. An essential partner-selection process negates overseas investment risks. By using commercial rights in existing business areas, Mitsubishi extended its earnings models at every stage of the value chain.

To quote the Jefferies Japan senior vice president Thanh Ha Pham, speaking to the *Financial Times*: 'The trading houses were written down as dinosaurs, but they are still around and making money here. They tend to evolve as businesses, and they do it well.' The prolonged success of the sōgō shōshas caught the attention of Berkshire Hathaway's Warren Buffett in 2019 and his revelation of this historic tool served to increase public awareness of the lending and investing options that exist and remain underused. What does this investment in sōgō shōsha mean for the future of trade investing?

The investments of Berkshire Hathaway

Warren Buffett and Charlie Munger's investment miracle began in the mid-1900s. After noticing a pattern in Berkshire Hathaway's stock price, Buffett watched the market and waited for the right time to purchase stock in a company. Whenever the company was forced to temporarily shut down a production mill, the stock price would initially drop. Once productivity resumed, the shares would soar again.

The next time a Berkshire Hathaway mill closed, Buffett requested to buy shares in the company. Seabury Stanton, running Berkshire Hathaway at the time, approached him to buy back his shares, but the agreement Stanton sent to Buffett undercut the deal so deeply that Buffett was furious. Instead of selling his stock to Stanton, he bought more, just to be petty. Nearly overnight, Buffett became the company's majority owner and fired Stanton. When Buffett made the purchase, Berkshire Hathaway was a failing textile business. By sheer determination and resourcefulness, the Buffett/Munger duo transformed it into a globally recognised, multibillion-dollar conglomerate.

Warren Buffett's preferred advice to investors is to watch everyone else in the marketplace and do the opposite. Wall Street calls this the contrarian approach. He didn't build a $652 billion company by following standard or even practical investment advice. Instead, Buffett looked for something different, something new or something previously undiscovered. When the Covid-19 pandemic hit, Buffett's Berkshire Hathaway was looking for new opportunities, not mulling over the past.

In August 2020, Berkshire Hathaway placed a $6 billion investment in Japan's five biggest sōgō shōsha trading houses. This investment was preceded by a dwindling number of foreign investments into SMEs, but Buffett's decision to invest in the sōgō shōshas marked a changing of the tide.

Buffett always looks past the present moment and peers into the future. Although the Japanese trading houses faced pandemic-related challenges like any other lending institution, Berkshire Hathaway's hundreds of subsidiaries and affiliates across all essential industries lowered the long-term risk. 'The five major trading companies have many joint ventures throughout the world and are likely to have more of these partnerships. I hope that there may be opportunities for mutual benefit,' Buffett said in a press interview to celebrate his 90th birthday in August 2020. Investors looking to diversify their portfolio with a low-risk asset in trade financing would do well to follow his advice.

The ability of the sōgō shōsha shows how long-standing these investments can be and how long they can continue to pay dividends. The relationship between SMEs and financiers is mutually beneficial. It helps both parties grow in a positive direction no matter what the financial market is doing, since trade financing today remains uncorrelated from the volatile stock market.

Generation fintech: Streamlining and speeding up processes

When trade finance began, exporters could not be sure when they would be paid for their goods by importers and importers struggled to work out how to securely pay their exporters. Paying for the goods before their shipments arrived was risky; what if the goods never came?

Paying for the goods after delivery meant that exporters might not receive their payments for sometimes months at a time, if at all, although letters of credit were partial answers to this problem. Modern technology reduced risk, but it remained a time-consuming process. The implementation of fintech will change trade finance as we know it.

No trade or investment is entirely risk free. Current technology improves the efficiency and safety of trades and for all parties. In the last century, trade finance traditionally relied on paper trails, telexes, emails and fax machines, which, after effectively pushing the telex out of use, are now more or less obsolete themselves. After decades of unrevised, lengthy trade-financing processes, the trade finance industry was ripe for an innovative leap, to handle trade in a more modern way. Fintech was born out of three quantum leaps which took place around the same time: technological advancements, the computing power of data analysis and financial overregulation. It can be summarised as a combination of AI, blockchain and machine learning, which make trade financing more straightforward and reliable.

The integration of fintech into trade finance was meant to provide a flexible and transparent resource to overcome the complexities of the past. Fintech is the financial terminology for describing innovative, technology-based financial products. Applications for consumer and SME-focused e-payment money-transfer systems, peer-to-peer (P2P) lending platforms and alternative currency exchange providers are all variations of fintech. With the invention of the blockchain and its cryptocurrencies travelling on it, global financial transactions could now be condensed into a single, decentralised platform, making trade financing easier even for SMEs to access.

By 2022, AI was used in most industries worldwide. Its application extends from industrial robots to self-driving cars and automated soda machines, as well as aeroplanes and rockets.

Fintech has unique AI qualities. Here are just a few examples of the most important uses of AI and machine-learning algorithms in finance: improved financial decision making; security and fraud detection; asset management; customer support; insurance; loans; forecasts; and personalisation.

As the platforms learn how to use financial-technology software, every transaction becomes increasingly quick and efficient. AI-powered scanners constantly learn what properties to look for, at the same time weeding out possibly fraudulent ones.

AI provides statistical predictions on buyer activities, customer trends and seller needs. This helps companies achieve their growth objectives and make them more relevant to their clients all while reducing operational costs and increasing internal efficiency.

Blockchains and cryptocurrencies are revolutionising trade

The best-known cryptocurrency has become a household name: bitcoin. Crypto is yet another fundamental driver of fintech. Platforms like PayPal, Square or Stripe are all considered fintech and are essentially the computer software that hosts the virtual delivery of web-based money for services. The value of the global fintech market is already valued at several hundred billion pounds.

Crypto wallets are themselves encrypted and not associated with names or bank accounts. The term 'crypto wallet' refers to a digital tool for securely managing cryptocurrencies by storing the private keys required to access them. But many fraud cases have shown that encryption alone is no guarantee against hacking and theft. Wallets should therefore be handled with the same care as cash in your pocket.

Blockchains are the business-delivery device of fintech. With the addition of blockchains to AI and crypto, fintech took off in the trade-finance industry. Transactions between lenders, buyers and sellers were streamlined, transaction costs were reduced, transaction timeframes were quicker and it introduced greater transparency and security for contracting parties through so-called smart contracts.

Blockchains store information on a redundant basis. Information can be transferred but never altered, deleted or retracted. In trade financing, it is common to exchange high quantities of documents and contracts per transaction. With fintech, instead of scanning and emailing 200 individual records, it is possible to transfer everything without multiple signatures and wait time.

The digitisation of trade finance had been slow but not due to a lack of demand. Cross-border trade involves much complex information, resulting in an overflow of documents, product details, transaction reports and point-of-sale paperwork.

Initially, the trade-finance industry worried that due to the complex nature of the workflow, the use of fintech was uneconomical for most trade deals. The first company to delve into the world of fintech for trade financing was Ornua, an Irish dairy company, in the form of a letter of credit (LC) transaction, using a digital fintech platform called Wave.

Wave was one of 11 fintech start-ups propelling trade financing into the twenty-first century with paperless dealings. Ornua was able to use the platform with ease on bulk milk deliveries. For Ornua to qualify for trade financing, it used Wave to have its LC approved by the bank and seamlessly received the money. Once the due date (the tenor) of the agreement was reached, Ornua repaid the investment received on the Wave platform and received the next round of funding for the following dairy shipment.

Ornua and Wave concluded that the differences between analogue documentation processing and fintech were remarkable.

Before fintech, it took Ornua 10 business days to receive an LC from the bank compared with just one day with Wave. Once the LC was approved, Wave automatically flagged the account for investors, triggering a payment directly to Ornua's business account.

Less than four hours later, $100,000 worth of cheese and butter was being transported from Ornua to an Irish-based food company. Along the way, Ornua investors could see the phases that the shipment was going through, including real-time approvals by the exporters and importers. They were also electronically notified when the shipment arrived.

The transparency that Wave provided to the investors was one of many unprecedented advantages of fintech. The benefits of using the technology in the trade-finance sector speak for themselves. It is not the only place blockchain systems have been shown to streamline trade deals effectively.

Fintech was also used to facilitate a trade-financing transaction between Australia and Japan in 2017 with the Marubeni Corporation. The agreement went through all the typical risk analysis and regulator checks using the new technology with great ease, exclusively using IBM's Hyperledger Fabric platform, with blockchain distributed ledger technology (DLT).

The new technology provided by IBM was built explicitly with DLT in mind. The infrastructure and protocols could be simultaneously accessed, validated and recorded across a network spread across multiple entities and locations. It effectively decentralised the process to allow for numerous moving parts occurring in tandem across the globe.

Both parties using the technology noticed faster document creation, transmission and delivery which cut both costs and time.

Again, transparency for both parties was increased, since the technology constantly gives a status update regarding shipments, deliveries and payment.

Meanwhile, Maersk, the Danish container-shipping giant, tested its blockchain solution to digitise its cargo inventories in Scandinavia. IBM ran a proof of concept (a test-run of the software) to ensure that this fintech application could handle demand. In September of 2016, Maersk, together with IBM, began tracking a container of flowers shipped from Kenya to the Netherlands.

The pilot programme ran on a blockchain network that the Marubeni Corporation had used. The technology was designed to support multiple parties across the global transportation system. It was hosted on the IBM 'cloud' and was an immediate success for both Maersk and IBM.

The introduction to this technology significantly reduced the delivery time for trade documents, cargo and related work tasks. Documents that had once taken several days or weeks to share and approve now only took a few hours, a breathtaking reduction in time to create and transmit documents and reduced costs through document digitisation. Importers, exporters and financiers saw transaction details in real time and could instantly share them with all parties involved.

Fintech in this application reduced errors in shipping documents and minimised, if not eliminated, the possibility of fraud. The blockchain system reduced product transit time and the shipping process; improved inventory management; reduced waste and the associated costs; and mitigated investor risk. The fintech system appeared to be working at multiple levels and for various industries, leaving the door open for other enterprises to follow suit.

These preliminary tests have proven largely beneficial and point towards a bright opportunity for fintech and blockchain in the trade-finance industry. The goals of this invention make trade more accessible for more investors. With the new forms of transparency and accountability from blockchain contracts, trade financing will attract a new generation of investors.

Trade financing has long been a reliable and profitable sector when managed prudently. The industry has witnessed substantial technological advancements that have enhanced its efficiency and security. Among the most notable innovations is the widespread adoption of smart contracts, which automate and enforce the terms of trade agreements, significantly reducing the need for intermediaries and minimising the risk of disputes. Integrating supply chain finance with the Internet of Things (IoT) has revolutionised the monitoring and management of goods in transit. IoT devices in shipments provide real-time data, enabling precise tracking, improved inventory management and more sophisticated risk assessments. These technologies streamline operations and unlock new avenues for financing complex global supply chains.

With enhanced risk-management protocols and the growing adaptation of fintech solutions within trade finance, even previously non-bankable trades are now becoming viable. Trade finance, once and still to some extent a niche sector, is steadily moving into the financial spotlight.

Experts anticipate that the continued integration of technologies such as blockchain, artificial intelligence (AI) and IoT will reshape the trade finance landscape, making transactions more secure, efficient and transparent. This presents unprecedented opportunities for investors to engage with an asset class that offers stability and innovation. As regulatory frameworks evolve, with an increasing focus on ESG compliance, investors will find themselves at the intersection of profitability and sustainability. The ongoing digital transformation, combined with potential market disruptions such as geopolitical tensions and shifts in global supply chains, is expected to create a dynamic environment rich with opportunities. By strategically positioning themselves in this evolving market, investors can capitalise on these trends, potentially achieving strong returns while contributing to the future of global trade.

Current trends: The boon and bane of increasing regulation

Before the 2020 pandemic, the 2008 global financial crisis (GFC) was cited as the most severe economic crisis since the Great Depression, which began in 1929. The early 2000s were again times of loose financial regulations, encouraging some of the wealthiest banks to take what appeared to the outside world to be unwarranted lending risks. This combination burst the housing bubble, tanked mortgages and forced respectable, global investment houses like Lehman Brothers, the fourth-largest US investment bank, founded in 1847, into liquidation.

As of 2024, the trade finance sector is confronting new challenges, particularly with the introduction of regulatory changes that prioritise sustainability and ESG compliance. These evolving regulations reshape how financial institutions finance trade, mandating a more vital adherence to ESG criteria. Institutions must now incorporate sustainability assessments into their financing processes, ensuring that their trade finance operations align with global efforts to address climate change and promote ethical business practices.

To prevent a collapse of the worldwide financial system in the face of the housing-market crash of 2008, governments around the world bailed out national financial institutions considered essential for the survival of their financial systems. Those were mainly banks and insurance companies with millions of customers and billions in deposits.

Global trade regulators also responded to the worldwide banking crisis. Prior to 2008, banks lent based on a host of criteria, varying from bank to bank and lender to lender. Then the global regulators decided that all banks needed to abide by the same lending restrictions within the framework of each institution and their product. With Basel II and Basel III regulations put into place, banks began focusing on lending only to SMEs with high credit scores and satisfyingly large capital-reserve requirements.

The financial institutions shifted their focus to larger corporate clients, abandoning lending to their SME customers. The move was to 'protect' banks from riskier lending options. This approach has slowed trade rebound and increased the gap between SMEs that needed trade financing and the availability of it. The $2.6 trillion worldwide trade-funding shortfall quoted in 2025 is felt the most by SMEs. World trade is in ever-growing need of capital.

The world's economies needed to prevent another global market crash; more regulations were the regulators' way of trying to prevent it. The global financial regulators thought that they were doing the nations a service. The new laws and regulations imparted to banks appeased the public in the face of government bailouts, an act on which citizens worldwide were staunchly divided. With restrictions on trade finance, emerging enterprises struggled to recover from the collapse, due to lack of capital.

The market would again go through turbulent times. In the face of a global lockdown, the world was on the verge of another economic collapse. The 2020 pandemic mercilessly uncovered and reinforced any simmering economic issues of banks and lending institutions. Some banks have greatly restricted their lending to SMEs, while others hardly lend to them at all or only against unrealistic debt coverage.

The unwillingness of big banks to lend affected the SME sector, accounting for over 90 per cent of most economies worldwide. With banks still refusing to lend, industries and economies continued to suffer. While trade must rely on the big banks, bank-related regulatory systems will continue to cause economic hardship for SME trade partners around the globe.

Education about trade and the financial market in universities appears much less applicable to the trade conditions in today's world. In response to the most recent economic downturn, many trade-industry participants, experts, traders and manufacturers hoped to see a reduction in trade regulations and a renewed commitment to their interests.

Trade industry leaders have always advocated for a decrease in global trade regulations, even more so now as economies which were barely surviving before the pandemic needed support beyond the traditional lending options.

The governments' principal claim against deregulation is that investing in trade finance is old-fashioned and risky when data visibly points to the opposite. This may have been true back in the early 1900s when trade financing started gaining popularity among local, wealthy investors. Statistics over decades confirm that financing trade is a low-risk and low-volatility investment.

Sensibly lowering regulatory overkill would provide the SMEs who need trade capital the most with funding and keep the global supply chain functioning. SMEs are a nation's instrument of economic growth and social development.

In most OECD countries, SMEs contribute more than 50 per cent of GDP. Some global estimates put this figure as high as 70 per cent. Thus, funding trade in times of economic uncertainty helps stabilise the global market and encourage worldwide economic growth.

Indeed, trade financing ties into the overall economy, though the trades themselves are not tied to the stock market. Trade finance investments do not shift with global market fluctuations; trade revolves around the need for specific goods and services imported or exported, making trade financing recession-proof and uncorrelated with the world's stock markets.

Even in times of downwardly spiralling global economies, trade-finance investments remained safe in times of economic distress. This phenomenon was proven over centuries by the thriving league of British merchant banks.

Chapter 3:

How Trade Finance Works: Methods, Means and Tools

Today, the most prevalent forms of trade financing include factoring, reverse factoring and supply chain financing (SCF). A more specialised approach involves investing directly within the value chain. In this chapter, we will examine these various methods in detail to understand how they operate, why they require the expertise of specialists, and how all parties involved – from exporters and importers to financing companies and investors – stand to benefit.

Not all trade finance operations work the same

Trade finance can be split into two broad groups: the high-quantity/low-value transactions with standard templates and highly automated processes, and the tailored transactions in our sector that require personal attention to undertake the individual business necessities.

Standard agreements are cost and time saving for bulk transactions. We are in the business of crafting individual agreements that support the borrower in the areas they need most. Our work is to ensure that every client and customer receives the best solution available, by providing a financial concierge service. This offers a thorough analysis of the specific business requirements to be matched with the most suitable type of agreement.

In the early stages, particularly of an international business relationship, there can be much apprehension by exporters working with new importers. Exporters can never really be sure that importers will pay their invoice on time or at all. Factoring and reverse factoring differ fundamentally from supply-chain financing. They are described in more detail below.

Factoring and reverse factoring

In factoring and reverse factoring, shareholders are investing in a credit-insured invoice as opposed to investing directly into the value chain. Buying credit-insured discounted invoices from SMEs is a cost-effective and straightforward way to finance SMEs in a secure way, bridging a lack of working capital or equity. A seller is now in the position to finance a larger shipment of cargo while still serving its current clients without any gaps in service or product supply.

Factoring: Buying an exporter's invoice at a discount

Factoring takes place when an investor or a firm like Artis buys an invoice from an exporter at a discount and receives the payment from that invoice by the importer on a pre-agreed future date. Factoring helps the exporter to collect payment sooner than the importer can provide it, hence optimising liquidity.

A good example is where a textile company needs to clear the current inventory at the end of the season, freeing up warehouse space for the next collection. The buyer isn't scheduled to pay the invoice for another three or four months.

The seller requires their working capital back as soon as possible, selling the invoices, often with credit insurance, at a discount and can use the cash flow to finance the next season's purchases. The importer still pays for the goods within the contractual timeframe.

You might think that factoring is a helpful tool for frontier, emerging or marginal markets – and it is, particularly for SMEs in most countries and across Europe. Discount margins vary strongly between and within regions, for example between European countries. In addition, each trade can be credit insured, reducing the default risk to a minimum. In 2021, Artis had a trade pipeline in Switzerland exceeding 1.5 billion Swiss francs. In wealthy Switzerland, you might wonder. Absolutely.

Currently, we favour short-term trade receivables up to 120 days. Other, often larger investment firms have different strategies. Some offer financing for up to one year or beyond, which requires a different risk assessment and often additional collateral. The next longer financing term is almost the same as project financing. When a trade financier finances the export of sugar cane or next year's sugar harvest, a project financier finances the sugar-processing plant. It is a different business and a different risk. We stick to trade.

Compared to supply-chain financing, factoring is a more streamlined process with fewer moving parts, people or documents. An invoice can be factored at any stage, from the pre-shipment process until after the product has already been delivered to the importer. Some companies factor invoices on 'future sales' where the buyer has yet not been identified. This is a type of risk that does not fit our business philosophy. Once the factor has purchased an invoice or a portfolio of invoices regardless of credit insurance and the specific parameters of the contract have been laid out, the exporter signs a sales/purchase contract with a factor including a discount.

The buyer pays the full invoice amount to Artis on the date due, regardless of when the goods are bound to be received. The arrangement is convenient for the sellers and the factor receives their margin for providing the funding. Buying the existing invoice minus the discount from the exporter locks in the margin upfront.

A factor is connected to in-depth financial and business information, including business databases, credit ratings or credit insurance that a seller often does not subscribe to or wish to pay for. For us it is money well spent.

Credit-insured invoices offer a high degree of protection against a buyer's inability or unwillingness to pay. While, ideally, sellers would have trade insurance on their buyers, not all sellers wish to purchase it. When an importer fails to pay, there is no formal protection for exporters and local sellers to recover their losses. The seller might have to go to a court in their own country or in a foreign jurisdiction, which might require dealing with the matter in a foreign language. With factoring, SMEs have guaranteed cash flow.

Another reason SMEs use factoring is to finance their growth. Growth financing can be a blessing and a curse as with the expansion of the company, not only does the invoice volume start to grow, but the raw-material-purchase bills to manufacture more goods grow as well. Rapidly growing companies may find themselves with more orders than inventory due to financial restraints. This is especially true when exporters' funds are tied up in late or slow-paying receivables.

A small steel manufacturer with low margins might require the buyer's cash to purchase the raw material to produce the product ordered. This can be a dicey part of the value-chain financing. When sellers can't service the needs of their customers, they might lose the business. The solution for manufacturers, provided they have the cash flow, is to pre-pay their suppliers for the additional raw material or parts to promptly fulfil all orders, thus keeping their loyal customers and providing inventory for the new ones.

While factoring is more straightforward than supply-chain financing, it still requires a healthy amount of risk mitigation and due diligence. The first step in the factoring process is the verification of parties' details. Factoring financiers wish to ensure that the seller requesting financing is in a legitimate business. The verification stage includes background checks, company history and overall reputation checks, as well as a review of the credibility of the importer.

Financial review and background check necessary

Financial reviews and background checks are essential components of validating an investment applicant. Recent advancements in digital tools have significantly improved the efficiency and precision of these processes. As of 2024, AI-driven platforms and machine learning algorithms are increasingly used to automate complex financial reviews, enhance credit scoring accuracy and streamline due diligence. These technologies enable faster data extraction and verification through tools like Optical Character Recognition (OCR), ensuring more accurate and reliable assessments. By thoroughly reviewing an enterprise's financial history, analysing annual reports and conducting background checks on key stakeholders, a factor can confidently ensure that the applicant is trustworthy and capable of repaying the investment.

Before an agreement is signed, Artis verifies the value of the product being factored. Once the sellers and buyers are both verified, it is time for personal due diligence. Artis project managers take trips to visit the company on-site to perform the audit. We look at the entire business process from production to shipment (ship, truck and plane). Investment firms invest large sums in purchasing invoices and it is the financiers' concern that the company will consistently deliver what the buyer has ordered from the importer, thus avoiding product issues upon arrival.

Artis reviews contracts in person and on-site. This minimises risks and misunderstandings when it comes to the factoring arrangement. Artis walks the exporter through the agreement in detail, giving the seller time to ask questions, address concerns or clarify. The parties must understand and agree to what is expected from each other in the transaction.

Once the exporter signs off on the contract, Artis owns the invoice of that shipment. Before the exporter is paid, Artis visits them. The buyer/importer is audited as well in a similar process.

A contact person from the importer is identified to address any issues with Artis during the process and until payment has been completed. The KYC (know your customer) process verifies that the customers are who they claim to be.

Once the payment is made to the exporter, the agreement is set in motion. The invoice and any credit and fraud insurance covers are transferred to the funder, who will monitor the deliverable and the payment terms agreed with the buyer. We prefer repeat business to one-off shipments, as the costs of setting up the relationship can be amortised over various deliveries. Artis tries to keep the tenors short – up to 100 days. The more quickly the product turns over, the sooner the parties get paid and the more product can be shipped.

Factoring helps SMEs manage their customer's credit and their cash flow. When an SME factors an invoice, the buyer owes that money to the investor and no longer to the seller. However, instead of the importer having a debt listed on their balance sheet's financial records, the invoice shows up in their account off balance sheet under 'trade payable' or 'accounts payable', which can protect a credit score rather than reflecting excessive debt on their financial record, if they pay their shipments on time.

It very much remains an obligation for the company; analysts often look at off-balance-sheet obligations as well. In factoring and reverse factoring, the credit line can be adjusted to the buyer's needs, provided their financials can support the increase of sales.

In a time of economic mayhem or decay, financial flexibility is a strong financial lifeline for a company. We saw businesses who typically paid their invoice tenor early or on time requesting payment extensions when the Covid-19 pandemic hit. The use of short-term factoring keeps thousands of businesses alive during economic hardships.

Factoring does not require the SME shareholders to give up any shares in their company or to sell or raise equity. Instead, it provides the factor ownership of a particular invoice only. The mission of a factoring company is neither to become a share-holder nor to run the company. The mission is only to improve the cash-flow situation of the company through factoring.

Reverse factoring: Same procedure, different initiator

Reverse factoring is initiated by the importer/buyer. It is best applied with solid, A-rated customers. Reverse factoring is not recommended in cases where the customer's credit quality is low-grade, or the proceeds are used to stretch deficient working capital.

Buyers favour reverse factoring to reduce the risk of supply-chain disruption. When importers have access to early payments, they are in a better position to honour their purchase due to the higher capital received upfront. With the funds transferred to the exporters on behalf of the importers, the exporter is keen to ship the cargo, reducing stock and freeing up space in the warehouse and cash. At the same time, buyers can grow their customer network without the added concern of a liquidity squeeze. Importers can sell the product in the market often before the invoice is due.

Reverse factoring increases the available working capital to importers. More working capital means that importers can increase the days payable outstanding (DPO). DPO is the average number of days it takes for a company to pay its suppliers and is a benchmark for investor and financing companies to determine the creditworthiness of a business.

A higher DPO indicates that a company takes longer to pay its suppliers. At least on paper, the company looks riskier. Especially during a growth phase, companies want to achieve a low DPO ratio, to remain attractive for new investors, proving legitimacy and reliability as a commercial party.

More working capital combined with a low DPO figure puts importers in a better position to negotiate with exporters. Importers who offer their exporters reverse factoring might negotiate more favourable commercial terms with their suppliers and get better trade deals and rates.

The process for reverse factoring follows the process for regular factoring as laid out previously. The same due diligence is done between the exporter, importer and their business connections. Once completed, the importer enters into a contractual agreement with the exporter and agrees on shipment volume and frequency. Subsequently, the exporter sends their invoice to the importer stating payment terms and conditions.

On receipt of the invoice, the importer submits the invoice to the trade-financing firm. The firm takes ownership of the invoice, including any entitlement to credit insurance, offering payment options to the importer/buyer ranging in our case up to 120 days. If the importer/buyer chooses to pay early, the finance provider will offer the importer/buyer a discount. Alternatively, the importer pays the total value of the invoice at the agreed payment date.

Walmart is a good example of a company using factoring and reverse factoring with suppliers. Becoming a Walmart vendor is a significant win for smaller exporters looking to generate more sales, hence revenue. This, however, can be a double-edged sword, as 'giants' like Walmart are known for placing massive orders but only allowing small margins.

It's the manufacturer's volume/margin dilemma. Such large orders can strain a smaller company that might not have the capital to meet the product demands ordered by a multibillion sales company.

The Walmart brand has always vouched for bringing products at the lowest price possible to consumers. Such promise still holds to this day, with the likes of Primark and Aldi promoting similar market philosophies. Large distributors sometimes sign big contracts with smaller, reasonably priced SMEs to find the lowest price for products.

Winning a mammoth order is one thing, but now the SME needs to finance the raw material, production and shipment. While we have been referring to Walmart again as an example, this applies, of course, to any large conglomerate with large distribution, hence purchasing power.

Two examples of (reverse) factoring

Artis was founded on the principles of logic, data analysis and responsibly contributing to more efficient trade worldwide, however small this contribution might be in a multi-trillion-dollar market. Our mission is not to champion or judge any specific causes, but we could not overlook a powerful illustration of (reverse) factoring demonstrated by a leading renewable energy company several years ago.

This illustration underscores the strategic role of reverse factoring in managing supply and demand fluctuations in a rapidly growing industry, providing you with crucial insights for your strategic planning.

The global demand for renewable energy solutions – such as solar panels and wind turbines – has surged in recent years. Major manufacturers, particularly in the solar energy sector, experienced unprecedented growth driven by global shifts towards sustainability and decarbonisation. In 2021 one of the largest solar panel manufacturers sought to expand production to meet increasing demand from corporations and governments investing in clean energy infrastructure.

Like other industries, large retailers and project developers typically operate on open-account terms, with payment cycles stretching up to 60 days. As demand spiked, this created a financing gap for manufacturers needing to scale production. The solar panel manufacturer turned to reverse factoring arrangements with an independent factor in this case. The factor provided the necessary capital to the manufacturer, enabling it to secure raw materials and ramp up production, ensuring that solar panels could be delivered on time to meet installation deadlines.

Depending on market competitiveness, large manufacturers in sectors like renewable energy can negotiate to reverse factoring for as little as one to two per cent of their margin over the standard rate. This potential for cost savings should inspire optimism and forward-thinking in your supply chain management strategies.

This arrangement allowed the solar panel manufacturer to manage its production scale, ensuring that distributors and project developers received the necessary equipment without delays. This financing method, by ensuring customer satisfaction, reassures you of its customer-centric approach in an industry where timing is critical – particularly when tied to government incentives and project timelines.

As with all forms of financing, factoring and reverse factoring carry inherent risks. Issues such as transport delays or damaged goods can arise but are often mitigated by insurance coverage. Timeliness is crucial in industries like renewable energy, where just-in-time supply chains are standard. Delays in equipment delivery can cause project disruptions, missed installation deadlines and extended financing terms due to delayed payments.

One more factoring illustration is meant to serve as an example of the immense benefits of invoice factoring in the face of internationally fluctuating supply and demand.

In 2017, the FBI reported more than 25 million firearm background checks linked to gun-purchase orders — more than a four-million-person increase from the previous two years. Major manufacturers like Smith & Wesson and Sturm Ruger were seeing record sales, in addition to major American firearm retailers including Cabela's and Dick's Sporting Goods, but it was Walmart who was leading the charge.

Walmart, a multibillion-dollar corporation, had one of the most significant years of firearm sales on record and the market continued to surge. In 2017, Walmart decided to apply reverse factoring. Large retailers around the world pay their invoices on open-account terms, requiring up to 60 days before remitting payment for the products sold. Why? Probably because they can. They place substantial orders. Take for example the food industry. If it takes two months for manufacturing and shipping, it could take up to 120 days before the manufacturer would receive a payment.

In our firearm case, Walmart did not want to advance the cash to manufacturers to finance their raw-material purchases. Instead, it sought reverse-factoring arrangements with an independent factor. The factor provided capital to the gun manufacturers to expand their production capabilities and keep up with the growing firearm demand.

Reverse factoring gave Walmart enough time to pay the invoices and helped to ensure that its shelves were stocked with products that its consumers wanted most – and immediately. Once a consumer decides on a purchase, they do not want to wait – and the seller knows the psychology of its buyer.

The timeliness for a delivery of products is of particular concern when the product is part of a just-in-time supply chain. A delay of just one day can mean stock and supply-chain disruption. Manufacturers and buyers depend on the punctual flow of parts in a world of lean supply chain with little stock in storage.

Timing and preparation for perishable deliveries are essential elements of a logistics and investment firm's verification and optimisation process. Then there is the risk of wrong delivery or non-delivery. It can take weeks for a shipment to be returned, (especially in international trade), and another delivery deployed to the importer. Importers are losing out on sales due to a delay and the tenor needs to be extended as importers might not have generated enough sales to satisfy the invoice.

A practical case of non-payment: Nevertheless, the financier's risk of loss is low

The possibility of not receiving payment is what keeps business owners, especially those of SMEs, awake at night. If the factor doesn't stay in touch with the importer, some rare importer may be tempted to 'forget' to remit payment. After all, the exporter has been paid and the importer received their goods. It is easy to ignore a faceless financier, particularly in a faraway country. To avoid such 'amnesia' we keep a close, face-to-face relationship with the businesses we are working with, for sellers and buyers to establish a personal partnership with our firm.

A new business that emerges in a market with competitive pricing can put pressure on profit margins for the current importer in pole position. When an industry or a market gains a new enterprise, the established companies must defend their market share. Many new enterprises will initially offer their product at unsustainable discounts, attracting a host of price-curious customers, a practice which is illegal. A factor's pending invoice might run into payment issues but credit insurance will take care of this.

To keep up with the new competitor on the block selling similar products at lower costs, other distributors might be forced to reduce their prices of that product line as well, unless they enjoy a privileged or monopolistic market position. Lower prices generally lead to lower margins, unless you can compensate for the loss by lowering your production cost, which in turn would mean inefficiency in the production process to start with. Necessity is the mother of all invention.

We, like others, apply a thorough credit assessment to mitigate internal and external credit risks. We do credit screening to confirm that the business has properly operated for at least two years. We want to see and understand a clearly defined purpose for the factoring need and ensure that our agreements are specific, clear and straightforward. The internal credit screening process ensures that the SME being financed can meet a minimum product turnover threshold. Does the company have a network of distributors to support that minimum product turnover? Do they have the suppliers to support the demand?

The internal credit screening takes a very detailed look at the creditworthiness of an SME, leaving no stone unturned. While we don't work from credit scores alone, we investigate whether a company is well-rounded, meets its projected goals and conducts reliable business within its industry and commercial networks.

In the effort to reduce fraud and money-laundering risks associated with factoring in international transactions, we execute a qualitative and quantitative risk analysis on the key owner(s) and senior managers. The current commercial value of the collateral needs to be checked, as it affects the quality of the debtors, suppliers and their financials. Old, obsolete stock and perished goods are worth much less over time than the initial purchase price. The internal credit check tests the recoverability in case an asset is completely lost.

Finally, all bank statements are reviewed by Artis's risk-management team, verifying the cash flow and ensuring that a single invoice has not been double financed. After completion of all internal screenings, the information is turned over to an independent third party for validation.

Third-party companies like Allianz Trade (formerly Euler Hermes), a market leader in credit insurance and part of the leading Allianz group, and others, independently verify all the documents provided by factoring and supply-chain financing companies before they confirm credit-insurance limits.

As a result, the credit-insurance company or credit agency will establish its own credit rating for the SME and assign a maximum factoring amount based on the buyer's financial records, cashflow receipts and sales records, limiting the risks on country and counterparty exposure. We check this information against our assessment to establish the terms of the factoring contract. A credit insurer can provide further trade-insurance options that cover bankruptcy, fraud and production errors.

Like trade financiers, credit agencies and insurers are not solely focused on exporters. Financing agreements, factoring limits and other terms are influenced by the importer's history. We want to be assured that an exporter delivers a good product and on time. Still, the financing arrangement is based on the importer's credit rating, not that of the exporter.

Statistically, factoring remains a very low-risk activity. Even in the face of the global pandemic that rocked the world economy, factoring remained a steady source of yield for exporters, importers and investors alike. While the rest of the world economy fluctuated almost daily amidst government shutdowns and financial strain, SMEs worldwide continued to buy and sell their products, some on a large scale. The success of online sales has been widely reported.

Grocery stores and home-improvement industries continued to boom not despite but because of the recent pandemic turbulence. Demand for cleaning supplies, toilet paper and other household goods went through the roof.

Many importers, investors and PPE opportunists did well. Factoring as an investment class is uncorrelated to the stock markets, so factoring deals also continued to thrive in the face of global economic uncertainty. Factoring has become a financial tool that businesses have leveraged to survive the recent economic turbulence; it proves to be profitable and successful time and time again.

Supply chain financing

The supply chain refers to transforming raw materials into a finished product ready for sale in any industry. For a pillow manufacturer, this journey includes sourcing textiles, filling, sewing, packaging, stocking, shipping and ultimately selling to the customer. Each stage of this process has its financing requirements, from the textile supplier to the packager and distributor. Supply chain financing encompasses various financial instruments, such as letters of credit (LCs), bank guarantees, financial guarantees and banker's acceptances, all of which facilitate transactions across these stages and ensure the smooth flow of goods from production to sale.

Tools used in supply chain financing.

Letters of credit (LC) can only be issued by banks, not by a commercial entity like a manufacturer or a trader. A letter of credit is the obligation of a bank to pay upon completion and confirmation of pre-agreed contractual terms. In recent years, there has been a significant shift towards digital letters of credit, which are transforming the trade finance landscape. These digital LCs leverage blockchain technology and other digital platforms to streamline the transaction process, drastically reducing the time required for document verification and approval. This not only speeds up transactions but also reduces the risk of fraud, as digital LCs provide enhanced transparency and traceability. Banks and financial institutions are increasingly adopting these technologies to improve efficiency and security, thereby making trade finance more accessible and reliable. The LC terms assure the buyer and the seller that payment shall be made if the services are performed as agreed in quality, quantity and time. Despite relevant paperwork, LCs remain a commonly used and trusted method for financing trade, securing both parties. Transactions and legal requirements are fulfilled through the bank. For financiers, the process is straightforward since the payment is guaranteed once the customer receives the LC from the issuing bank.

Bank guarantees (BGs)/financial guarantees: These are financial instruments issued by a bank, an insurance company, or another financial institution that guarantees that an agreed-upon amount will be paid to a financier at an agreed-upon date. Recently, regulatory changes have been introduced to adapt to new market conditions, particularly focusing on enhancing transparency and security in international trade. For example, the European Union's Digital Operational Resilience Act (DORA) of 2024 includes provisions that impact the handling of bank guarantees by mandating stricter digital reporting and monitoring requirements. This shift aims to reduce the risks of fraud and operational errors in cross-border transactions, ensuring that financial guarantees are executed with greater reliability and accountability. Such regulatory adaptations are crucial in the current global trade environment, where the complexity and volume of international transactions continue to grow. Unlike an LC, the sum is only paid if the counterparty in the transaction did not fulfil the stipulated contractual obligations. Thus, a BG is a mechanism that protects a buyer or seller against losses that might occur due to the non-performance of the other party. It is a layer of protection after the fact rather than an LC which acts as a bank-backed 'I-owe-you-and-I-pay-you'. While generally an appropriate tool to protect a transaction in some jurisdictions, BGs can only be executed after a favourable judgement.

Banker's Acceptance (BA): A banker's acceptance (BA) is a form of payment guaranteed by a bank rather than an individual account holder, ensuring payment at a future date. Traditionally used in international trade, BAs have evolved significantly with fintech innovations, particularly in emerging markets. Fintech platforms now utilise advanced algorithms and blockchain technology to enhance the security and reliability of BAs. These digital tools allow real-time transaction tracking and verification, reducing fraud and error risks. In markets with less developed financial infrastructure, fintech solutions make BAs more accessible and dependable, fostering greater confidence among trade partners. These technological advancements are driving a resurgence in the use of BAs as fintech continues democratising access to trade finance in previously underserved regions.

As noted earlier, trade credit is a subset of trade financing. Trade credit defines the payment relationship between importer and exporter. When an importer and exporter or a buyer and a seller get into a contract together, the seller might expect to be paid within 30, 60, 90 or even 120 days from the date the buyer receives their goods.

In many (European) countries, the buyer has the choice to pay the bill in full within 10 days and deduct a two per cent discount from the total amount – often referred to as *skonto* – or to pay the bill on the due date without *skonto*. A two per cent discount for 10 days does not sound much but is substantial on an annualised basis.

Trade credit has become a popular tool among trade investors for its margin, safety and ability to preserve cash flow as the business grows. Exporters and suppliers can generate more business without demanding cash up front. Financiers receive a margin and often ask for collateral from the buyer to protect themselves. Even though there isn't a bank involved in the lending process, the buyer still risks added fees and interest if not paid on time, just like any other financial agreement might require.

The best illustration for trade credit comes from a store that has grown into an international powerhouse across 20 different countries today: Walmart. Walmart did not start off as 'American made'. When Sam Walton first sought to start Walmart, his goal was to deliver the best goods to the American people at the lowest cost possible. To do that, he had to buy the goods as cheaply as possible, which often meant favouring imports. American-made goods were proving to be too costly for Walton.

Early in his company's enormous expansion, he decided to set up trade across the Pacific to make importing a pillar of the Walmart business model. Walmart at the time was still an SME. Looking to expand its company overseas was a big jump that required more capital than he had access to.

The good news was that Walton didn't have to do it all on his own. Walmart was showing promise as an enterprise and was making waves but was still a relatively new business in the early 1980s. Instead of pooling together just enough Walmart money for his first international trade coming out of the Pacific, Walton was able to make use of trade credit with a trade financier and the desired exporter. Walmart negotiated to buy the low-cost imports that they required and paid for them later.

Exporters out of the Pacific were happy to begin working with Walmart, a company on the rise, but they operated strict trade credit in the beginning. Exporters provided the goods under the 'net 60' terms, meaning that Walmart had to pay the entire balance 60 days after receipt of goods. If the balance was paid within 10 days, there was a 20 per cent discount available. If paid within 30 days, the discount decreased to 10 per cent. When Walmart received the goods, it sold them to its customers with its margin and consistently paid the balance owed ahead of schedule, giving the company a better margin.

According to a confidant, Walton himself estimated that imports accounted for nearly six per cent of Walmart's total sales in 1984. But Frank Yuan, a former Taiwan-based apparel middleman who dealt with Walmart in the 1980s, puts the number, including indirect imports, at around 40 per cent from the start. Either way, Walton's vision was a harbinger of far more extensive global sourcing today.

The 2019 Small Business Credit Survey found that trade credit finance is the third most popular financing tool used by small businesses. Yet the SMEs taking full advantage of this business-to-business lending option don't tend to stay small- or medium-sized for long. Trade finance has led to the enormous growth of economies across the globe as it has bridged the financial gap between importers and exporters. An exporter is no longer afraid of an importer's defaulting on payments; an importer is sure that all the goods ordered have been sent by the exporter, as verified by the trade financier.

The pandemic had a monumental impact on the global economy and revealed several inefficiencies in the trade-financing industry. Weaker capital reserves and bargaining power have hurt the ability of SMEs in developing countries and emerging or frontier economies to get efficient trade-financing facilities and they are subjected to higher associated trade-financing costs. Banks prefer to work with more established, so-called large-cap companies.

With the lack of support for SMEs during this pandemic, the World Trade Organization (WTO) has raised concerns that underdeveloped nations and financial systems could be left out of the trade-finance markets. The most vulnerable sections of the trade-finance market should be getting more flexibility and funding through specific programmes designed to help emerging economies survive a pandemic. Business-to-business/ P2P lending continues to provide greater flexibility to businesses struggling to obtain financing from the financial sector, despite a valid and collateralised trade.

Investing in the value chain

So far, in this chapter, we have looked at factoring, reverse factoring and supply chain financing via trade credit. However, anyone who wants to maximise profits and minimise risk in this business cannot avoid taking a closer look at what is being financed – i.e. the traded goods. The value chain offers a great opportunity to optimise trade financing and profit margins. And here, another method can be added, namely financing with direct collateralisation by the goods in question.

The product you are currently holding in your hand might be from another part of the world. How did it reach you? Which parts of the value chain are worth investing in?

Banks used to be the primary lender for SMEs looking to sell into new markets. Since the early 2000s, more trade-fund specialists have emerged. These firms are often focusing on specific sectors or geographies. One fund might specialise in Uzbek trade only; many focused or still focus on Africa, financing trade or harvest. Another does Cuba only, and a Florida-based trade fund finances bicycles for Florida residents. Horses for courses, so to speak. An interesting case we are pursuing is financing the export of Uzbek textiles to German buyers. Our factoring clients are the German importers. High margins, 1 per cent per month combined with a German risk is quite rare.

While the above-mentioned might be easy investments for a local Uzbek or local Florida-based investor, they are complex, if not unsuitable, for foreign investors – Artis included. All resides in the fund manager's expertise, which led us to adopt a focused approach.

As there are various ways to participate in financing trade, so there are various parts of a trade that can be financed. All parts of a trade combined constitute the value chain.

The value chain is defined as a series of processes that a specific firm or industry undertakes to transform raw material to a product of value and sell to the final customer.

In 1985 economist and Harvard business academic Professor Michael Porter coined the concept of the value chain. In trade finance, the value chain is essential for investors to understand and make informed investment decisions at each level of the value chain. With each production or manufacturing stage that the product passes through, its economic value should increase.

The overall process of moving a product through the value chain to eventually be purchased by a consumer is referred to as the value system or industry value chain. From raw-material sourcing to transportation, the industry value chain also includes third-party contractors and suppliers providing necessary support as a product shipment travels through the stages of the chain.

Artis has experience in facilitating trade-finance arrangements at different levels of the value chain. We focus on certain parts of the value chain and exclude others. Today, Artis does not take on the financing of agricultural production or the shipping of perishable foods. In addition to our practical experience, our trade process has evolved with the market. It is key to adapt to the needs of our clients as they grow.

The four primary levels of the value chain are: input, production, processing and distribution. Our philosophy is to provide capital to the buyer/importer at the latest and safest stage of the value chain. An optimised value chain makes businesses more efficient and delivers the highest-value product at the lowest costs.

The input phase is the very beginning of the value chain. This is where the raw materials are acquired from external suppliers and sources. Inbound-phase value-chain activities include buying, cleaning, receiving and storing input pieces for the production process. Suppliers require pre-shipment credit or an open account.

A girl's best friend: Diamonds are a good example

Let us look at the inbound phase in the precious-stone or diamond industry, which begins with sourcing the raw diamonds. In the input phase, workers source the raw stones from the earth. The value of the plain, uncut stone may vary but from this point, value keeps being added to the product.

Next comes the production phase. Artis does not typically get involved in production. In this phase, the raw materials are prepared, modified and assembled. There isn't much for us to finance at this level as it requires working capital, customarily provided by the company's own funds (equity) or bank loans.

In the production phase, the raw precious stones, which could be diamonds, emeralds, rubies or aquamarines, to name a few, are cut by specialists. Raw diamonds are romantic but not widely sought after by paying customers. The diamond's true romance resides in a sparkling cut, brilliant colour and perfect clarity.

Diamonds today are cut primarily in Belgium, India and Israel and significant financial value is added once this stage is complete – or destroyed should the cut fail. It is the superbly cut stone that makes diamonds a girl's best friend, at least according to Marilyn Monroe's iconic movie song. Minute imperfections or a flawed cut devalue the priciest stone.

Now comes the processing phase. In this phase, multiple materials from various industries are combined in a single location and assembled. In our fictitious, precious-stone business, loose stones are put together to create a piece of jewellery, such as an elegant ring, a glittering necklace or a breathtaking pendant. This phase often requires a variety of talents to bring the product together – goldsmiths for engagement-ring settings, for example. Delicate chains are delivered complete with clasps and polished ready for use. For this stage of the value chain, funding is required to purchase parts or more materials. In the processing phase, trade finance uses open accounts, which are often reimbursed in less than 30 days. All parties rely upon speedy trade and reliable deliveries.

The final phase is the distribution stage. After the product or service has been packaged, bundled and perfected, it is ready for distribution and customer purchase. The distribution phase includes warehousing, logistics, trading and transport.

The levels of return vary by industry but hinge on the level of the value chain that is being financed. Not all levels in the value chain are equally financially attractive to outside investors. As the entire value must be funded, it is the obligation of the company to ensure adequate financing across the whole value chain. Broken value chains do not produce a saleable product.

Learnings from supply chain disruptions in the past

The COVID-19 pandemic exposed the fragility of global supply chains, making supply-chain disruption a critical issue worldwide. The sudden halt of international trade in early 2020 was particularly dramatic, with small retailers bearing the brunt due to a lack of contingency plans.

In the aftermath, long-term changes have emerged, with companies increasingly adopting localisation and nearshoring practices to reduce lead times and enhance supply chain resilience. Regions such as Mexico and Eastern Europe have become vital hubs for production as businesses aim to bring manufacturing closer to home. This shift has opened new opportunities for trade finance, with financiers adapting to these more localised supply chains by offering flexible, customised financing solutions. At Artis, we recognise the importance of risk mitigation in trade finance. We refrain from engaging when open credit arrangements prove unsuitable or excessively risky for exports. Instead, we extend the working capital cycle for importers at multiple levels of the value chain, ensuring open accounts offer the highest security for both enterprises and investors. For exporters, we shorten the working capital cycle by providing pre-shipment advances, a strategy that mirrors the security and profitability of import financing with open accounts.

It's worth taking a close look

Value-chain investing upholds the entire value system, impacting global trade and the world economy. For investors, it is essential to understand how the value chain works, so that you can be de-risked and ultimately funded.

The parts of a value chain that are habitually funded are: the equipment required to operate; mining or extraction where appropriate; manufacturing; purchase of raw material; the process of converting raw material into semi-finished or sellable goods; and the process of bringing the sellable goods to the market.

With each funding opportunity there are subparts that can also be funded. Each possible investment, however, has a different risk and return profile even if you are looking at different parts of the same level in the value chain.

Even though trade-finance companies ensure that risk is mitigated to the utmost degree, a residual risk remains which can cause problems to arise. An unreliable trucking company or logistics company can bring an entire supply chain and sales cycle to a halt.

The impact of the 2021 semiconductor shortage on the car industry provides a vivid example. Without each piece available, production halts and the delay ends up costing all participants of the value chain. One slip-up affects the chain and ultimately the brand's reputation. For established large enterprises, such production delays might be financially digestible, but SMEs or emerging markets don't have the cushion of additional resources and workforce to help alleviate such pressure.

Let's revert to our precious-stone business. In the diamond industry, the diamond itself is rarely the final product, except for collectors; diamond jewellery is the final product.

Every delivery driver and company that employs them needs to be reliable. Every dock shipment needs to be guaranteed and every cargo count needs to be uniformly trustworthy. Reducing the risk of fraud or theft in the trade-finance industry remains a top priority. As we know now, trade finance used to be rife with fraud before technological advancements of the twenty-first century and it has been reduced dramatically with the implementation of fintech. In addition to those advancements, rating agencies have helped to evaluate the parties being financed to demonstrate the level of reliability of that company.

Various regulatory bodies were enacted as early as 1913 with the creation of the US Federal Reserve System (in short:

The Fed). The idea behind regulatory agencies was to create transparency within a somewhat opaque system. Regulatory agencies can make it easier for investors and SMEs taking on financing arrangements.

The history of an enterprise is another key factor considered by rating agencies. An all-inclusive view of the people running the business which we intend to finance is pertinent. Rating agencies take the enterprise's history a step further, also looking at the industry in which the company operates. This includes the company's projected impact on a particular industry and on the economy. Rating agencies validate the SME looking for financing from a third party, so investors, private or corporate, can proceed with confidence that the business will honour its financial obligation and repay the funds borrowed.

The Fed today is still the most influential of all policy-making monetary bodies and its influence stretches around the globe. Its decisions are closely monitored by banks, corporations, markets and governments. The Fed is often criticised in the media for influencing monetary policies, credit conditions and overall lack of liquidity in the worldwide market. As much as the Fed comes under scrutiny for its work, the board also makes its fair share of positive market contributions. The Fed supervises the US banking system and in extremis the international banking system and helps provide stability to the financial markets, also overseeing other regulatory branches.

The process that trade finance companies undergo before onboarding a new borrower is rigorous and extends beyond mere risk assessment or financial considerations, as will be explored in chapters 6 and 7. Investors are increasingly focused on companies meeting acceptable environmental and social responsibility (ESR) standards. ESR has become a crucial benchmark for investors and borrowers, reflecting a growing commitment to ethical and sustainable business practices.

Our pre-deal evaluation criteria include whether a company has an ESR policy in place, for example is going 'green'; is aiming to become carbon neutral; undertaking water saving and recycling initiatives; composting onsite; using renewable energy; and cooperating with other socially responsible companies.

This includes paying workers living wages or ensuring that everyone from truck drivers to dock loaders have appropriate working conditions. From responsible farming to trustworthy manufacturing, responsible investors request that their money is helping responsible business owners to create sustainability for their merchandise and their workers.

Consistent with a recent ICC trade register report, trade finance has an average default rate of 0.02 per cent across the entire global trade market. The same report found that, on average, general (non-trade) lending is five times riskier than trade-finance lending. The combination of international regulators, rating agencies and the trade company's proprietary due diligence on both borrowers and lenders make this process as secure as it can possibly be.

For the reader new to trade finance, all of this – the multiple moving parts and the different levels of the value chain may seem somewhat overwhelming. While it is essential to understand how each level works, it is as important to keep it simple.

As a trade-finance investor, you are invested in one of the levels of the value chain by either supplying a pre-shipment advance to exporters or an open account to importers. In either arrangement, the importer and exporter can get the capital they need upfront and repay later.

Artis's approach to financing trade receivables

Artis aims to consistently achieve above-average and stable returns by investing in one of the most secure asset classes available – trade receivables. These trades are sourced across an extensive, established network of local merchants and global suppliers, primarily in Europe, Central Asia, the Middle East and Africa.

Artis focuses on enterprises with clear developmental potential, established relationships with buyers, a proven track record of delivering products and meeting the highest quality standards in their respective markets, but are underappreciated by banks.

Our investment strategy is centred around receivable financing, with a focus on reinvestment, business continuity and avoidance of spot transactions. As a sector-neutral trade financier focusing on non-perishable goods, our strategy provides diversification of exposure across sectors and a conservative approach to risk mitigation.

Multiple trade-finance statistics back up the status of the trade finance asset class as an 'uncrowned king' of low-risk, low-volatility investment. Together we will sift through the industry track records and our own to provide ample evidence of the reliability of this asset as well as looking at the cost of a trade investment.

Is a trade investment still worthwhile and are there hidden fees?

As an investor, you look out for the overall cost of an investment. The same applies to trade-finance investment and potential costs should be discussed and disclosed. There can never be enough risk mitigation; our proprietary credit-assessment process ensures that this is always the case. Our model is based on deep financial analysis and forecasting of the industry and enterprise.

The process includes qualitative risk analysis with a thorough background check on the business owner and management in addition to a balance-sheet audit for creditworthiness; marketability and debt capacity; fraud-risk analysis; and third-party credit rating.

An on-site visit is essential to make sure that the goods in question are not simply a figment of someone's imagination.

A credit-assessment intake form is completed by the applicant and analysed by our team. The collateral is assessed and our risk analysts determine the level of account recoverability.

The internal application process for the terms of the financing arrangement can be accepted, rejected or altered by the firm any time before the agreement is signed.

We complete an in-depth analysis of the risk, which includes making sure we consider any targeted countries and industries. Finally, Artis checks the quality and standing of the applicant's debts and their relationship with suppliers.

As a regulated firm investing in trade, we maintain a high level of value across the board. Every investor can expect a professional set-up with highly educated, trained and experienced team members. Our risk managers' experience is comparable with any found in a large financial company in the City. Our trade lawyer is on a par with a partner of any of Europe's large law firms. A detailed and time-intensive work analysis is undertaken to investigate each transaction before selecting and executing the chosen few.

There is a cost of doing business. Artis, like other companies, charges a management fee. This fee helps to compensate our team for the high-quality work we do on the ground with clients and extensive back-office paperwork. In addition, we levy a defined percentage from the overall returns.

Investors might be tempted to avoid the fees involved in working with a trade-financing firm in order to maximise returns.

There is nothing wrong with that, though the experienced guidance of a dedicated and knowledgeable team protects your investment and should not be underestimated.

Much value lies in the ability to manage and mitigate risks that arise along the transaction chain. It is all about structuring deals for protection, ongoing account monitoring and control of the transactions towards eventual settlement.

This often makes the difference between a successful finance arrangement and failure and is the prime reason why a premium is justified for the fund managers.

The value of a team

A systematic and rigorous approach to risk assessment and a checklist approach is vital to achieve low risk and must be followed scrupulously. Our value-based approach to trade financing is a proprietary model founded on our qualitative and quantitative criteria developed over the years.

One might think that the drivers in the trade-finance industry are the same as everywhere else – business risk, operational risk and credit risks. While it is essential to consider these risks, they are not the main transaction drivers in trade, which are negotiation, market competition and positive business relationships. In addition, there are the discretionary factors. Discretionary factors have historically remained unanalysed, which explains the inconsistencies in trade financing pricing.

Trade Works

Shouldn't transaction drivers have a larger weighting than trade-financing pricing? In this school of thought, field discretionary factors are not weighed as heavily in respect to trade pricing.

After reviewing many transactions over the past 10 years, the Boston Consulting Group found that it is the field discretionary factor that influences the trade-finance pricing and not the transaction drivers.

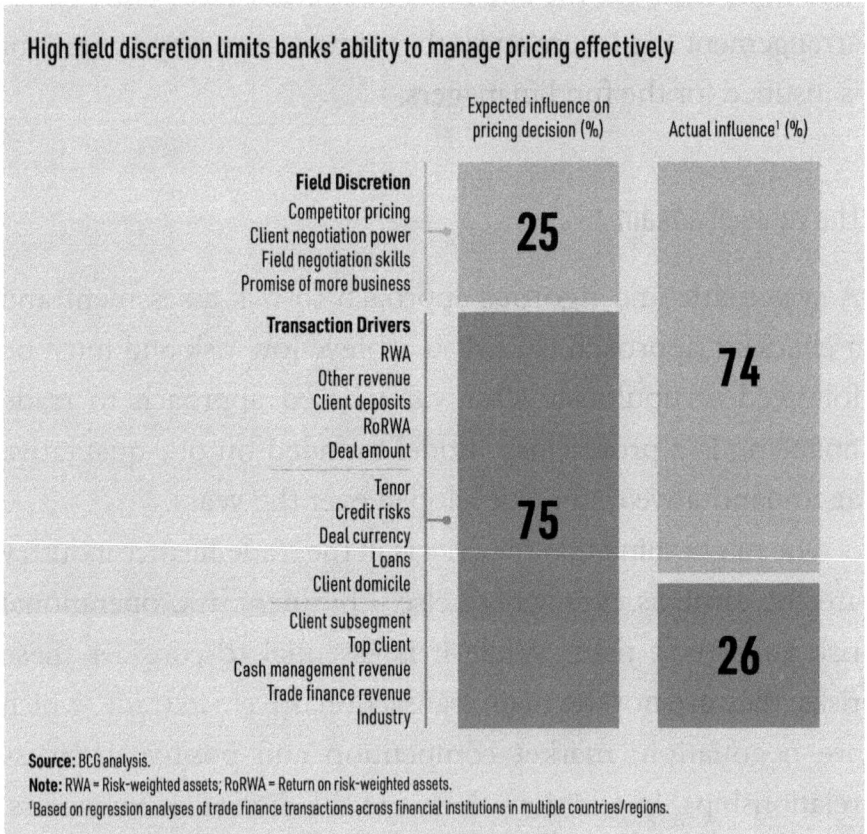

High field discretion limits banks' ability to manage pricing effectively

	Expected influence on pricing decision (%)	Actual influence[1] (%)
Field Discretion Competitor pricing Client negotiation power Field negotiation skills Promise of more business	25	74
Transaction Drivers RWA Other revenue Client deposits RoRWA Deal amount Tenor Credit risks Deal currency Loans Client domicile Client subsegment Top client Cash management revenue Trade finance revenue Industry	75	26

Source: BCG analysis.
Note: RWA = Risk-weighted assets; RoRWA = Return on risk-weighted assets.
[1]Based on regression analyses of trade finance transactions across financial institutions in multiple countries/regions.

Source: Sumitra Karthikeyan et al., 'Breaking the Commodity Trap In Trade Finance', BCG Global, 2019. https://www.bcg.com/publications/2019/breaking-commodity-trap-trade-finance

Trade and trade-finance professionals rely on their established, proprietary networks and make frequent visits and enquiries to protect their investment. The 'boots-on-the-ground' approach of our team members is vital, wherever we invest.

The benefits of a tenor

The investment tenor – the number of calendar days until the maturity of trade – has become increasingly dynamic with advancements in trade logistics and digital contract management. Modern technologies such as AI-driven analytics and blockchain enable real-time monitoring of supply chains and automated contract enforcement, allowing for more accurate predictions of delivery times and better risk management. These innovations have led to shorter, more reliable tenors and the ability to swiftly adjust them in response to market conditions or logistical disruptions. As a result, trade finance investments have become more secure and efficient, benefiting both investors and businesses.

The decision on the tenor date depends on the type of trade, industry, value chain and other specific factors for each deal. At Artis, we accept tenors ranging from 30 days for open accounts to a maximum of 120 days for various account types. This short trade cycle aligns with our strategy, reduces the duration of outstanding cash and creates consistent reinvestment opportunities. We grow alongside the businesses we finance.

Trade Works

The combination of credit-insured receivables and short redemption periods positions Artis's trade investment as a viable alternative to short-term bank deposits. This blend of short maturities and lower risk is a winning formula for high and stable profits.

Tenors are influenced by global market demand and competition. For high-demand products like mobile phones, tenors are typically shorter, as the companies being funded are in growth mode. Conversely, industrial products like pumps have longer tenor cycles. Companies entering new markets may seek extended tenors to build momentum or offer their buyers more flexible payment terms, allowing them to pay for products with sales proceeds rather than from their reserves.

This chapter has shown that trade finance offers many opportunities to generate profits with the correct methods, means and tools. However, the individual tailoring of each transaction determines its profitability and the magnitude of those profits. Caution is key. Speaking of caution, trade finance also has darker aspects and there are, and always have been, bad actors in the industry. That's the focus of the next chapter.

Chapter 4:

Gamblers, Crooks and Spies:
The Dark Side of Trade Financing

With regular repeats of financial crises over the years, each asset class has its controversies, gossip and juicy stories. Some people in politics, administration and public life have a bad opinion of trade finance, associating it with money laundering and monetary shenanigans. This generalisation is incorrect. But there's a need to take a closer look at what went wrong in the past. Let's peek at the darker side of the trade-finance industry.

Research-driven investors discover trade finance as a financially appealing and protected asset class, providing funding to meet the growing demand for financing trade. Financing trade ideally carries a social responsibility. Regulators believe financing international trade attracts money launderers and other financial wrongdoers as well. Such generalisation can easily be applied to any coffee shop, dry cleaner, bakery or amusement park — in fact any place that exchanges products or services for cash (i.e. where large numbers of transactions are undertaken, for small amounts of money). The same cautious methods the banks enact as protection can be adopted by investment firms as well.

The case of British merchant banks offers ample evidence of what happened when trade financiers failed to mitigate risk properly and, thus, learned the hard way, through financial or existential loss. A particularly shocking case was the burning up of a stellar name: Barings.

The fall of Barings Bank

Barings Bank was founded in 1762 by Francis Baring, a British-born member of the German-British Baring family of merchants and bankers. Its collapse in 1995 after trader Nick Leeson was promoted to run its Singapore office shook the financial world.

Leeson joined the settlements department of Barings Bank in London in 1989, having learned the art of trading in futures (buying or selling a commodity at a specific price and date in the future) in Japan.

At the time, Barings Bank was one of the most established and reputable banks in the world. Leeson was working predominantly in assets like commodities, precious metals, stocks and bonds. He was excellent at his job and quickly climbed the ladder within the bank. He seemed to be making money for the bank and his superiors liked this personable and driven young man. At 28 he was promoted to head of the Baring Bank office in Singapore.

Leeson executed and settled transactions through the Singapore Exchange, but he did not invest in trades at all; he was merely guessing about and betting on industries and trades which would be profitable using derivatives. This seemed to pay off for the bank, with his transactions accounting for nearly £10 million or 10 per cent of its annual profits.

As the Singapore office director and as per his instructions, Leeson should have kept the books cash neutral, managing investment portfolios without adding any of the firm's capital. Capital gained or lost on a trade belonged solely to the client's account, with the bank taking a brokerage fee as compensation for facilitating the trade, regardless of the economic outcome.

Leeson – claiming later that he was bored – began using the bank's capital for his market bets. Time and time again, the market worked against him. His situation became desperate and his investment motivation each day was to recover the loss of yesterday – a reckless double-up strategy, more suited to Las Vegas where it is called a martingale. The snag with this strategy is that if you run out of cash you lose. This is what happened to Leeson.

While all this was happening, his employers still trusted Leeson because they didn't know what he was up to, and he seemed to be making a significant and positive financial impact on the bank's profit and market reputation. He should not have been left with the responsibility of checking his own trades.

Instead, the bank should have supervised him, advising him to safely balance his risky investments.

Leeson hid his bad trades in a fake account which became known as the '88888' account. It recorded all the trades and losses Leeson funded with bank equity carefully hidden from Baring's headquarters in London. By 1993 Leeson was down over £23 million; within a year, his undeclared and unaccounted losses stood at £208 million.

On 16 January 1995, Leeson was desperate to earn back the money he had lost. He decided to play a 'safe' hand that day. Expecting that the markets and therefore his options would remain stable overnight, he decided to straddle the Singapore and Tokyo stock markets.

This strategy is used when the trader believes the underlying asset will not move significantly higher or lower over the lives of the options contracts. The maximum profit is the amount of premium collected by writing the options, but the potential loss can be unlimited, so it is typically a strategy for more advanced traders. The risky move would allow Leeson to recoup a small number of losses that he could reinvest and start making substantial amounts of money back.

That night his position in the market was conservative and the stock market remained stable, but overnight, the Great Hanshin-Awaji earthquake hit Japan and caused the Asian markets to collapse. The large-scale quake hit the Ōsaka-Kōbe (Hanshin) metropolitan area of western Japan; faced with even more enormous losses, Leeson attempted to offset his trading failures by investing in a series of increasingly risky trades betting on the recovery of the Singaporean market. But these market trades didn't pay off either. With discovery now inevitable, Leeson fled to Kuala Lumpur with his wife.

Barings officials launched an investigation into his activities and discovered the 88888 account with losses of £827 million, all of which Barings was liable to cover and which was twice the bank's available trading capital.

There was no conceivable way to save the bank. Following a frantic and failed bailout attempt, on 26 February 1995 and 233 years after it first traded, Barings Bank ceased to exist. The same day, Leeson was arrested in Germany and charged with fraud, deceiving his superiors and inappropriately allocating bank funds.

Lessons learned from Leeson

The lessons that the world trade sector learned from the disaster were that no one person can be responsible for nor should be allowed to check and approve their own trades, and that every industry must have checks and balances built into the system, protecting the global economy and investment firms alike.

With trade-finance arrangements spanning continents, time zones and cultures, not to mention the complexities with documentation, logistics and compliance, daily trade risks and issues to watch out for are often on a much smaller scale than espionage or criminal intent.

Fraud in the context of trade financing is the purposeful mis-use and abuse of financing trades for illegal or immoral purposes. The intended outcome is deception, which can happen in a multitude of ways.

Money laundering

Money laundering has become a permanent concern — and not only in trade. The act of money laundering is when agreements are made to conceal the origin of funds.

The Global Trade Review stated in an August 2020 article: 'International trade networks can attract criminals who exploit the interconnected supply chains to move illicit funds through the formal financial system, a practice known as trade-based money laundering' (www.gtr.com). The prevalence of criminal schemes has grown as well in the trade-finance sector and the results are lengthy and increasingly costly processes.

Importers and exporters can also be victims. For example, a business or an individual based in a country called Atlantic Europa, (the fictional country in *The Tale of Eliminating Bandits* (1847), one of the sequels in *The Water Margin,* an early Chinese novel) is sitting on cash collected by selling illegal or sanctioned products or selling to sanctioned countries. To recycle the funds and make them legitimate, the fund owners invest in a trade-financing arrangement.

Once the invoice is settled, that money comes back clean. Criminal organisations and syndicates today own significant industrial and real estate in most countries. They take great care to come across as legitimate SMEs. Global regulators have difficulties telling the difference between the funds and the owners. While regulations are vital for organised business, overregulation strangles it.

Impersonation

Impersonation is defined as when parties conceal their identity and it often goes together with money laundering. Not all that is not disclosed is fraud, of course; there can be many reasons why beneficiaries do not wish to disclose transactions, contracts or facts. The most valid one is personal discretion, a none-of-your-business approach I personally very much defend.

On the less glamorous side of the impersonation spectrum are bankruptcies, unsuccessful banking and business history, and credit ratings. The dark side of the (trade) moon.

FATF, the Paris-based Financial Action Task Force founded by the G7 countries in 1989, is a global standard-setting body working with financial intelligence units across the globe, cleansing the legitimate trade-finance sector of money-laundering and impersonation schemes. FATF works in conjunction with Europol, the European Union's law-enforcement agency.

A recent success of FATF and Europol was the shutdown of a multinational money-laundering network in 2020. The agencies found that a trading network involving car parts was laundering money for local drug traffickers and tax evaders. The criminal activity was supplemented by false paper trails for sales and purchases to disguise the funds' origin and confirmed ties to the Mafia. Blending the illegal with the legitimate trading activity, the corrupt business intended to evade detection and hide its criminal activity under cover of legitimate transactions.

Fake trades

Fake trades appear in a company's official business and financial records but never actually happen in real life. False documentation to gain approval for trade-financing arrangements is a widespread issue. Blockchain technology offers a possible remedy.

False documentation includes fake invoices; false LCs and bank guarantees; and well-crafted but false bank statements and balance sheets. It is impressive – and somewhat concerning – to see what can be created with a high-end colour printer.

Double financing

Double financing is the term for when a company receives funding from more than one investment firm for the same invoice, cargo or receivable. The result is that funders are not paid for goods as the importers are not receiving them.

A case of double financing rocked the industry in early 2020 when Asian markets started to struggle with the Covid-19 pandemic and oil prices plummeted. This combination created a liquidity squeeze.

As lenders attempted to collect payments, cracks widened in the exporter's balance sheets. By March 2020, when Credit Agricole SA and HSBC Holdings PLC issued a payment guarantee for $76.5 millions of fuel from a Singaporean trader, Hin Leong Trading Pte., they had no idea that they would be the newest victims of a double financing scam. While Hin Leong Trading Pte. was pledging the fuel to back the loan, it alleged agreed to sell the same cargo to another trader, who sought letters of credit from three banks, including Credit Agricole. When the issue was investigated, the Singapore police discovered that they overstated the value of assets by 'an astonishing amount of at least US$3 billion' comprising US$2.23 billion in accounts receivables which had no prospect of recovery and US$0.8 billion in inventory shortfalls.

An illegitimate activity often is the last effort to generate liquidity and to cover the company's financial losses. The double-financing schemes focus on the sale and repurchase of a cargo.

Funds received from one financial institution were allocated to a previous customer's account to inflate their receivable balances. The result is a kind of trade-financing Ponzi scheme, and the process needs to be repeated to keep the enterprise afloat until the bitter end. To continue the farce, the enterprises in question falsified financial and business documents on a massive scale to obtain their financing. As of June 2020, global regulators had identified 15 banks and 58 import letters of credit that were not supported by an underlying sale or transaction. The debt amounted to US$3.5 billion.

The practice of double invoicing came to life in the 1980s and is primarily possible due to a lack of due diligence on the part of the borrower or, alternatively, is an inside job. Experts lean towards the belief that the trade-crime issue in Singapore was an isolated incident.

The fraud allegation against several Singapore trading companies led to a downturn of the Singapore economy that rippled into other financial economies worldwide. The market has given rise to the question of whether those scandals are isolated incidents provoked by rogue traders, a trade-finance problem or a Singapore problem. We can avoid future repeats by performing extensive due diligence.

Authenticity of goods and 'swag'

People dealing in stolen or illegally purchased goods for profit are called fences. Luxury Swiss watches, often Rolexes, are sold at a ridiculous fraction of their price because they are either an imitation or from a theft — either way, defrauding tourists or international jewellers. It does not take much commercial wisdom to question the true origin of a Rolex sold for €25 on a street corner or even for €999 as a special deal.

Authenticity is a rising problem for premium-goods manufacturers as the margin between a genuine Rolex and a fake are dramatic. In certain markets there are even fake Porsche cars still sold as Porsche, let alone the fake Lacoste crocodile logos, as well as Hermès and Louis Vuitton handbags, to name a few of the most obvious examples.

The three critical things which may happen when offered cheap goods are: they are of poor quality; there is late delivery or no delivery at all; or the goods are damaged or incorrect on arrival.

The Greensill case

Supply-chain financing firms experienced significant receivable problems in 2021. Greensill, an Australian investment firm founded in 2011, had a meteoric rise, becoming an international leader in supply-chain financing, with over €160 billion in assets financed.

With offices in London, New York, Chicago, Miami, Frankfurt and Sydney, and banks in the UK and Germany, Greensill served corporate customers in over 60 countries. The investment firm came under scrutiny when Germany's financial-supervisory agency, BaFin, noticed irregularities and asked law enforcement to conduct a special forensic investigation into Greensill's German bank.

The 2021 run-in with the law was not the first time that Greensill came under regulatory scrutiny. In May 2020, BaFin reported that several of Greensill's clients defaulted amid large-scale corporate collapses and accounting scandals, as reported by the *Financial Times*. In 2020, Greensill quietly leaned on its insurers to cover the losses and hoped that the industry wouldn't notice.

To get a sense of scale, the *Financial Times* reported that investment funds had close to $120 million of exposure in the troubled firms, including firms like Agritrade, another Singapore-based commodity trader and BrightHouse, the British rent-to-own and cash-lending service company.

BaFin, as well as the UK's Financial Conduct Authority (FCA) and Serious Fraud Office (SFO), audited Greensill's financial records, paying particular attention to the account of one of its largest borrowers, the UK-based and Indian-owned GFG Alliance conglomerate, a noteworthy owner of UK steel companies: 'One of the most serious findings of BaFin's probe was that the bank booked claims for transactions that hadn't yet occurred, but which were accounted for as if they had', Bloomberg reported, citing people familiar with the matter. The questionable claims were related to companies associated with British industrialist Sanjeev Gupta, a key client of Greensill Capital.

While the investigation continued, the major insurer that covered Greensill globally, not the individual invoices they discounted, withdrew their two most significant policies. Without such blanket insurance coverage, Greensill was unable to continue operating and filed for insolvency. Tarnished by criminal accusations of false receivables and a still-ongoing investigation by the UK Serious Fraud Office, no other investment firm was willing to or interested in taking on the risk associated with the protection of potentially a no-product or no-goods situation.

In the US, Greensill was found to have been lending money to SMEs based on potential future sales of a business, instead of on its past transaction history, which heightened the level of risk and could be interpreted as an irresponsible approach to financing international markets and good-faith investors.

Greensill's loss in insurance coverage triggered a wave of defaults among Greensill borrowers, causing the losses of more than 50,000 jobs worldwide. The company's collapse was swift and final as the administrators looked to liquidate its assets. Greensill attempted to sell the financing company to another investment firm to ease its losses. The *Financial Times* reported that BaFin also filed a criminal complaint against Greensill's German bank management for suspected balance-sheet manipulation – the final nail in the proverbial coffin.

UBS settlement and investor recovery in August 2024

The aftermath of Greensill's collapse continues to unfold while another drama happened: Credit Suisse, a major Swiss bank founded in 1856, was sold to its competitor UBS in a dramatic sale in 2023, ending a 167-year-old tradition.

In summer of 2023 UBS decided to settle the substantial losses tied to the Credit Suisse supply chain finance funds. Once praised as a bright star in the sky of secure investments, the Greensill funds left about 1,200 investors grappling with uncertainty when Greensill Capital's unorthodox financing practices came to light and revealed that Greensill had extended financing far beyond what it had declared, ultimately leading to the loss of $10 billion in assets.

Several lawsuits have been filed against UBS and the Government of Switzerland related to the Greensill Capital scandal. Parties involved creditors of Greensill Capital including major institutional investors, Greensill Capital's liquidators (seeking claims related to the bankruptcy), regulators and government entities (for compliance and regulatory issues), and investors and clients who suffered losses due to the collapse of Greensill Capital.

In a strategic move to restore investor confidence and close this devastating chapter, UBS, which inherited these troubled funds with the acquisition of Credit Suisse, has offered in summer 2024 to buy back the affected fund units at 90 per cent of their original value as of 25 February 2021. This offer provided investors with a rare opportunity to recover most of their investments.

While UBS's 90 per cent reimbursement offer was most likely motivated by reputational, legal and possibly Swiss political considerations it is in line with the broader historical performance of trade finance as an asset class. Trade finance has consistently demonstrated low commercial default rates, often cited as being under 1 per cent. According to the International Chamber of Commerce's Annual Trade Register, default rates of trade related finance products, including letters of credit and supply chain finance were less than 0.25 per cent! Such resilience is rooted in typically short-term and self-liquidating trade finance transactions, backed by tangible goods and services.

Lessons learned from Greensill

The Greensill Capital collapse offers profound lessons for the trade finance industry and its investors:

- **Due diligence and risk assessment are paramount.** A rigorous evaluation process is essential to succeed in trade finance. This means conducting thorough due diligence on financial products, counterparties and underlying assets. Risk must be assessed, monitored and managed at every stage of the transaction – not just those associated with complex financial structures or leverage.

- **Ensure transparency.** Transparency in financial reporting and the mechanics of trade finance instruments is non-negotiable. At Artis, we've invested in a bespoke risk-management system that provides daily visibility into every aspect of a transaction for all stakeholders. Equally important is the understanding of product complexity: a complete comprehension of the underlying transaction and its financing mechanism is crucial to mitigate risks.
- **Regulatory compliance is essential.** Adhering to stringent national regulations and industry standards is fundamental to preventing mismanagement and fraud. Staying informed about regulatory changes ensures ongoing compliance and positions firms at the forefront of best practices.
- **Verify creditworthiness and asset quality.** The quality and authenticity of financed assets must be rigorously assessed. Thorough credit analysis of borrowers and intermediaries is critical to avoid over-reliance on inflated credit ratings.
- **Mitigate counterparty risk.** Diversification is vital to avoiding an over-concentration of risk with a single counterparty or product. Monitoring counterparties' financial health and stability helps maintain a balanced risk profile.
- **Strengthen internal controls and governance.** Robust governance structures and internal controls are

indispensable for overseeing trade finance activities. At Artis, we conduct quarterly assurance reviews that feed into our annual audit, ensuring we adhere to best practices and proactively identify areas for improvement.

- **Foster communication and education.** It is crucial to educate stakeholders on the complexities and risks of trade finance. At Artis, we offer open access to our publications via our website, promoting transparency and informed decision-making. Clear communication channels between investors, counterparties and regulators reinforce trust and operational clarity.

Navigating the complexities of trade finance with clarity

In the wake of Greensill's collapse, the trade finance sector has come under intense scrutiny. Investors are now more cautious, seeking firms that promise validated returns and demonstrate an unwavering commitment to transparency and risk management.

At Artis, our approach to trade financing is rooted in a philosophy of transparency and rigorous oversight. We focus exclusively on financing genuine, legally binding transactions – not speculative trades. This ensures that every deal we undertake is underpinned by tangible goods or services, significantly reducing the risk of default.

Our risk-management strategy is comprehensive and robust. Every trade receivable we finance is backed by credit insurance from investment-grade insurers such as Hermes Trade or CESCE, the latter of which is state-owned by the Spanish government. This arrangement provides an investment-grade uplift to our transactions, offering a critical safety net covering up to 100 per cent of potential losses.

The downfall of Greensill underscored the perils of opacity and unchecked ambition in trade finance. Managing scalability without compromising financial and operational integrity is vital in this complex sector. At Artis, we remain steadfast in our commitment to these principles, ensuring that our operations are profitable and built on a foundation of trust and sound governance.

The involvement of banks

Red flags began popping up in 2021 around billions in Paycheck Protection Program (PPP) loans that seemed illegitimate. This is a business loan programme in the United States set up by the Trump administration in 2020 to help companies continue paying their employees' salaries during the coronavirus pandemic. As of April 2021, the US Justice Department had brought criminal charges against 209 individuals in 119 cases related to the PPP. It has been alleged in criminal charges by the Justice Department that one SBA (Small Business Administration) employee took bribes to process fraudulent economic-injury disaster loans.

As well as seeking to bribe banks, criminal companies might attempt to entice trade-financing firms directly to provide money for felonious activity if they agree to turn a blind eye. However, with governing bodies increasing their audits, these incidents tend to happen less. As a result, while trade finance becomes more regulated, overall cost per transaction increases.

Non-payment

Non-payment can occur for a multitude of reasons, including lack of funds by the buyer or lack of intent to pay their invoices. It might also occur when SMEs enter larger markets with more competitors offering the same products at lower rates. Emerging SMEs may need to lower their prices, decreasing their margins, leaving them with less liquidity to honour their invoices – in other words, market share at any price. While not always directly fraudulent, there is an inherent fraud risk involved.

Artis's strategy for avoiding fraud and unfair practices

Being highly thorough in the choice of markets, sectors, counterparties and investment opportunities is imperative. The goals are simple; to mitigate risk and to apply enhanced due diligence.

Adequate governance is in place at Artis and ensures observance of these principles.

Internal processes have been established to reduce our reliance on external risk assessment, including detailed appraisal, transaction optimisation and double verification of everything from personal histories of upper management through to the network of suppliers that both importers and exporters use to conduct their business.

Appraising the customer in depth requires full business transparency by the borrower. Artis wants to know if and where the transaction adds value. Agents not adding value to the product chain are often a red flag and to be avoided.

The basic rules we like

1. Speak to the person paying for the product. While this might kill many so-called opportunities, it saves significant time, money and nerves. It eliminates much of the unknown from the outset in particular deals that only existed in the mind of an intermediary and without commercial validation.
2. Monitor the profit and loss trends of the business and how they perform in a flourishing and declining market.

Companies withholding information, records or histories won't be funded. The more open a company is about sharing personal and business information with Artis, the more easily the firm will move to the next stage of verification.

Optimising the transaction and trade

We craft our contracts with risk mitigation in mind. Minimising risk leads to the decision as to whether a lender requires supply chain financing or factor. At this stage, we decide on pre-shipment payment or offer the SME an open account. Optimising the trade case by case means more control, less risk and predictable returns for investors.

Other methods to optimise and verify a trade outside the inherent trade structure include the physical inspection of the trade collateral. There are many good inspection companies that assist in this process, so you do not have to visit each warehouse.

An optimised trade results in the appropriate tenor and satisfactory payment terms for all parties.

The importer will thus have enough time to pay for the product and benefit from better liquidity management, while the exporters will have pre-shipment funds available to facilitate seamless transport of goods; an optimised trade is therefore a trade worth the investment.

The inspection

The next stage in the process is to inspect all documentation and any third-party confirmations. Issues that could have been missed during the first verification stage might be found by simply carefully re-reading documentation and combing through the small print.

Secondary inspection steps we take include verifying the signatures to ensure that they match across all documents. A personal signature tends to vary slightly with each stroke of the pen. The review mechanisms need to be state of the art to identify even small details.

The legal due diligence is a must and is undergone before signing off on any contracts and paying any funds.

Once financing is deployed, audits continue to be performed at regular intervals. Regular audits of the accounts spot payment delay early. A deal approved three months ago may not be due for payment for another two months; much can happen in five months. Auditing our assets at regular intervals prevents the risk of double financing, leaving the firm without payment on significant invoices or without delivering the promised goods.

Timely reminders

In the face of delayed payments, we take the same methodical approach as we do in our due diligence. Trade-finance companies are here to support their clients in difficult moments. It is in the interest of all parties, especially after putting them through extensive legal and operational checks.

The collection of our invoices begins with a notice of the invoice payment 15 days before a payment is due, leaving the buyer enough time to arrange for liquidity planning.

If payment is not received by the tenor date, Artis will be in touch again with a reminder. In the case of factoring, Artis reminds the borrower that they are the owner of the goods and claims the return of the goods. If payment reminders continue to go unanswered, Artis will enact other means of getting the attention of borrowers, to expedite payment.

A single transaction can be made up of various small invoices. Invoice payments that are more than seven days overdue are reported to the major credit bureaux, which might prevent the borrower from obtaining funding until the matter is resolved.

A claim is filed with the credit insurance to receive payment from insurance instead of relying on the borrower. The final stage is for Artis to discontinue funding of the account and file for the insurance pay-out for the total amount of the transaction. Our insurances cover fraud as well as port risks, delivery failures and other problems.

We have acquired our knowledge from our history in the trade financing sector and from seeing the mistakes that other financing institutions have suffered from. Next, we will look at the legal sanctions and challenges associated with international trade that can impact investments for years to come.

Chapter 5:

The Risks in Trade Finance

In the previous chapter, we explored the darker side of trade finance, highlighting the dangers posed by unscrupulous actors – crooks, spies and bad-faith players – and outlined strategies to mitigate these deceptive practices. Now, we shift our focus to risks unrelated to fraud. Two primary categories warrant attention: political risk and the risks stemming from supply chain disruptions.

The political risk

Sanctions generally have a devastating effect on trade, a result that is very much part of the calculation of the sanction issuer, be this a nation or an international body, for example the UN or the EU. Political risks to the trade industry often stem from simmering geopolitical tensions (Middle East), military issues (Ukraine), human-rights issues and child labour to name a few. Political risk affects local and international trade and supply.

Dramatic examples with dire results for the civil population are the long-standing sanctions against North Korea, Syria or Iran, where the lack of bank payment facilities suffocates basic trade, often including products for survival – food and medicines. The sanctions that countries impose on each other are a moral failure of societies.

Trade sanctions are not a modern invention. Napoleon Bonaparte found his own continental blockade system extremely helpful. The embargo which banned British ships from entering European ports was applied intermittently, ending on 11 April 1814. Napoleon could not enforce a boycott through all European countries and extensive trade continued throughout Spain and Russia, so he invaded both countries. Overall, the blockade caused little economic damage to Britain, although British exports to the continent (as a proportion of its total trade) dropped from 55 per cent to 25 per cent between 1802 and 1806.

The legal force of national and extraterritorial sanctions could prevent a company from receiving or issuing a letter of credit (LC), collecting on funds or fulfilling confirmed, even prepaid orders. Credit insurance should shield exporters and investors from this risk.

Public, private or hybrid credit insurance exists for most markets at competitive prices. Even today, some provide coverage for countries like Afghanistan and Iran. Public credit insurance is the insurer of last resort and a government tool to encourage national exporters to sell beyond their comfort zone. Political risks are a quasi-permanent concern when dealing internationally, especially but not only with frontier markets.

Even with detailed research and stringent protocols in place to structure and finance a transaction, residual risks to bear in mind remain, particularly along the supply chain, like an incorrect or damaged product arriving at a distributor.

We mitigate these risks using LCs, bank guarantees, trade credit insurance and our proprietary risk-mitigation process.

Then there is always the 'black swan', the unforeseen, such as the default of a customer on its loan. Artis has had none so far. Insurance and collateral are there to mitigate the remainder of the risks of default. When a customer defaults, the credit-insurance company is informed immediately and will take over the handling of the recovery process, a process that involves all parties. An alternative to factoring individual invoices and reducing industrial or political receivable exposure in bulk is to sell an entire package to a trade financier at a discount.

The supply chain risk

Political risks, often translating into commercial risks or losses, remain a concern when dealing with frontier markets. While research, checklists and processes mitigate risks, there are micro risks to be conscious of, particularly in the supply chain.

A typical supply-chain issue is when the product is delivered incorrectly or arrives at a distributor damaged. While it can feel like the end of the world for all the parties involved, these risks are mitigated using LCs, trade credit, transport insurance and our own extensive risk-management process. In these situations, investment firms can also use insurance and collateral to mitigate the remaining default risks.

When companies have difficulties paying an invoice on time, a trading or trade-finance house can often provide more flexibility and act faster to restructure payment and avoid default. Banks are often less agile due to stricter lending terms, inflexible payment dates and multi-jurisdiction sanction registers to respect.

Going into default on traditional business loans can have dire consequences for the business, creating unnecessary losses for the company, trade partners and shareholders. Trade-finance firms can use additional collateral to shield themselves against unprotected losses.

Example: An overnight import ban as a pretext for non-payment

We don't often get involved in issues of clients defaulting on their payments, but I want to share one example. A few years ago, our firm, Arjan Capital, had to navigate our client out of a truly terrible lending situation. It was the non-payment of an open-account trade, which means delivery of the goods comes first with payment later.

Sounds crazy, I know – to trust your client without collateral. A flock of black swans, one might think. But the black-swan excuse does not hold as the risks were known, understood, recommended against and explicitly accepted by the exporter. So, what happened?

The client was a multibillion-dollar fast-moving consumer goods (FMCG) company with significant export experience in frontier markets. We had an advisory role and were also involved in the handling of the transaction, including logistics and payment. Our financial obligation was fiduciary only. We paid to the seller what we collected from the buyer after deduction of our fee.

The sales manager wanted to access this potentially large market that was difficult to access at all costs, selling imported premium goods into the nation's many pharmacies, with a market structure not unlike that in France. Similar products were being produced locally under international licences at half the cost. To be fair, the quality of locally manufactured product was often inferior to the imported original. The country was and still is in an economic 'pickle' and the consumer's purchase decision was mainly driven by price not quality.

Multiple market analyses confirmed a promising outlook for this large and up-and-coming frontier market. The first deliveries went well. There were some delays due to unclear and changing customs import rules and complex payment situations due to currency controls.

Our client's buyer was either unwilling or unable to produce an LC, either because they were trying to save the 1 per cent LC cost or simply did not have the funds available, hoping (remember Sam Walton) to pay the supplier after he sold and collected on the product.

We kept telling our export client to ship only either against prepayment or at least with some collateral – for instance, LC or credit insurance. Even a personal cheque would have helped. Product or money-recovery procedures were unclear and the rule of law is largely untested by international firms.

The exporter's sales desk and his superiors decided to provide the buyer with unsecured trade credit of about €250,000, the value of an average shipment. To receive the next shipment, the previous one had to be fully paid for.

The black swan in this situation was that to preserve foreign currency and to fight inflation and unemployment, the importer's government decided overnight to ban the import of thousands of finished goods, leaving countless container loads stranded at the border or perishing in warehouses. Products could only be imported either in parts, also called SKD (semi-knocked down) or as raw material but not as finished goods, apart from whatever the country did not produce internally.

For reasons of quality control, our client decided against delivering anything other than finished and packaged goods. Raw material in bulk and packaging locally was not an option either. This decision was communicated while the shipment was sent out but not yet paid for, and the importer knew that this was the end of the commercial relationship.

The goods had about two years of shelf life left. With the shelf life ticking away, goods were losing value every day. Shipping back to Europe was unreasonably costly, so the importer sensed the opportunity to force a farewell discount from the seller. On the one hand, we had a reputable European multinational seller, on the other side a competent but financially weak and small importer.

The buyer felt that the legal system in his frontier market would protect him as a local company and discourage the foreign seller, hence he took a rather high-handed approach.

We cautioned the buyer that the multinational seller would pursue him in court in his home country in case of non-payment. After negotiating for weeks and weeks, the seller agreed to a very generous 40 per cent discount, to get paid and to get out. The discount amount offered was in the low six figures.

We mutually agreed on a payment date and a daily penalty with a cap of 60 days in case of further non-payments. The buyer paid 85 per cent on time and then stopped again. We reminded him that the multinational would legally pursue the remaining 15 per cent, and he was at risk of an arbitration case where his 40 per cent discount could be invalidated. It was to no avail. After 60 days of further non-payment and the required formal notices to the buyer, the seller filed in arbitration for the full amount, including penalties. For the seller, our legal expense was an investment with a potentially high upside; for the buyer, a large downside only. We could not understand the buyer's reasoning, risking 40 per cent discount plus penalty payments and legal costs instead of paying the remaining 15 per cent.

As I mentioned, such incidents are rare at Artis; in this case, we only played an advisory role. Nevertheless, we are committed to learning from past mistakes. We thoroughly analyse each incident, driven by the belief that past missteps pave the way for future successes. In the next chapter, we will take a closer look at how we approach risk management.

Chapter 6:

Managing Risks: Legal Requirements and Voluntary Safety Measures

R isk management involves legal obligations and voluntary actions that a trade financier should adopt in its interest. In this chapter we will explore both aspects. First, we will examine the regulations primarily affecting banks. As discussed earlier, the growing wave of regulatory burdens has made it increasingly challenging for them, prompting many to withdraw from the trade finance sector.

Non-bank trade financiers are also subject to specific legal requirements, though the regulatory intensity is considerably lower. Solid measures are essential to avoid misconduct and payment defaults, whether mandated by law or not. These practices, which we will also cover in this chapter, are critical to ensuring success in this business. Meticulous implementation of these safeguards has been a cornerstone of our achievements.

Legal requirementse and the Basel Framework

Investments in any asset class must operate within local laws and regulations. In the post-Brexit UK, trade finance faces an increasingly complex regulatory landscape, which has become even more intricate with the latest developments in the Basel Framework. Basel IV, expected to be fully implemented by January 2025, introduces more refined methodologies for assessing credit risk, significantly impacting the trade finance sector. These reforms aim to improve the precision of risk-weighted asset (RWA) calculations, compelling financial institutions to hold additional capital against high-risk exposures. The implications for trade finance are substantial, as these rules may restrict access to capital, particularly for SMEs, while fostering more robust risk-management practices across the industry.

As we established previously, prior to 1988 banks primarily regulated themselves. A careful attitude by the management or partners with unlimited liabilities – a legal form that has essentially disappeared apart from some rare banks in places like Switzerland or London – obviated the need for extensive laws and regulations on how to issue loans or credit to private or corporate borrowers.

The industry knew how to manage itself until some lending institutions and banks got themselves into trouble through increasing margin chasing at the expense of stringent loan requirements and management of due-diligence processes.

The first global standard requirements for trade originated from Germany's largest insolvency after the Second World War, that of the Herstatt Bank in June 1974, an infamous incident which clearly illustrates the issue of settlement risk in international finance.

The Herstatt scandal sent a shiver down the spine of the so-called 'Deutschland AG', the German network of banking and industry, and led to the creation of the Basel Committee on Banking Supervision (BCBS), a committee with representatives from central banks and regulatory authorities, charged with finding ways to control risks and address issues caused by systematic flaws and regulatory shortcomings.

The bank was closely tied to the international financial markets, and its collapse triggered an economic downfall that echoed around the world. It prompted global coordination to prevent a recurrence of such disruptions of the credit market.

The coordinated efforts resulted in the Basel I agreement, which established globally applicable requirements and regulations for trade financing.

The financial sector swiftly adapted to these new laws, and sanctions imposed by international regulators forced the committee to react once more. In 1999, the BCBS put in place the second set of regulations – Basel II – to crack down on the amount of fraud and legislative shortcomings in international trade and to address the pitfalls of current trade-financing practices.

Once it gained momentum, the committee didn't stop and Basel III was created in response to the 2007–08 financial crisis, detailing the principles for appropriate risk management and account supervision. The new set of regulations was designed to respond to the overwhelming lack of liquidity buffers in the face of the US housing-market collapse.

In 2017, the Basel Committee finalised its post-crisis reforms under Basel III, introducing new standards for calculating capital requirements for credit risk and credit-valuation adjustment (CVA) risk. Subsequent evaluations by the Basel Committee on Banking Supervision (BCBS) and the European Central Bank (ECB) have examined the effectiveness of Basel III in enhancing the resilience of the global financial system. The BCBS's 2022 evaluation report concluded that Basel III has strengthened bank resilience and reduced systemic risk by raising capital and liquidity standards. However, the report also highlighted potential unintended consequences, including increased capital costs for banks, which could limit lending, particularly to SMEs. Similarly, the ECB's 2023 analysis confirmed that while Basel III has contributed to more excellent financial stability, the transitional costs of implementation, though moderate, were necessary to secure long-term benefits.

Many of the lawyers, economists and political participants who developed and calibrated the Basel regulations found their efforts to some extent insufficient as they could not prevent the financial crisis of 2007–08.

The economic crisis unsettled banks and resulted in a severe credit 'crunch' and a series of government bailouts of unprecedented scale. After the most urgent crisis management was completed in 2009, the idea of international trade-regulations work was taken up again.

In the wake of this financial crisis, the BCBS published nearly 3,000 pages, covering more than half of the entire regulatory framework. The Basel Framework has reached a whole new dimension. The document today serves as a framework for international trade finance and sets the standard for operations.

There are three categories of legal measures that financial institutions must respect and investors should be aware of: system regulations (large-scale measures across the industry to organise trade in general); prudential regulations (which focus on the institution's financial health and oblige financial firms to control risk, hold adequate capital, maintain liquidity requirements and monitor large exposure); and non-prudential regulations which are independent of the financial health of the regulated institution.

These regulations include: the permission to lend; transparency regulations; consumer-protection regulations; AML laws; KYC laws.

The following diagram outlines the development of the current Basel III framework. The second diagram shows the historical development of US financial regulations in comparison.

	2011-2013	2014-2016	2017-2019	Basel III current status of implementation
After the Global Financial Crisis of 2008, the Basel Committee on Banking Supervision (BCBS) decided to strengthen the Basel standards further. The Basel standards were introduced in December 2010. Basel III standards were revised and enhanced in different phases from 2013-2019.	2011: Improvements in the calculations of the capital requirements 2012: Counterparty standards introduced 2013: Introduction of liquidity coverage ratio (LCR) 2013: To start implementing Basel III into EU regulation, the Capital Requirements Directive (CRD IV) was introduced.	2014: Net stable funding ratio (NSFR) was introduced. 2016: Bank for International Settlements (BIS) adopted the fundamental review of the trading book (FRTB). Introduced in the aftermath of the 2008 financial crisis, the FRTB is a worldwide set of rules that specify the minimum regulatory capital requirements for banks' wholesale trading activities. 2016: BIS adopted interest-rate risk in the banking book (IRRBB). It is part of the Basel capital framework's Pillar 2 (Supervisory Review Process) for the management and supervision of interest-rate risk (IRR). 2016: Capital Requirements Regulation II (CRR II) proposed, containing FRTB and IRRBB 2016: Implementation of leverage and liquidity ratio for small banks 2016: Revised market-risk framework of Basel III published	The Basel Committee's oversight body, the Group of Central Bank-Governors and Heads of Supervision (GHOS), mainly supervises the implementation of Basel frameworks. GHOS finalised Basel reforms at a meeting on 7 December 2017. The main objective was to make the overall banking system more resilient around the globe, especially for EU member countries. At its next meeting on Basel reforms, on 14 January 2019, GHOS further enhanced the market-risk framework. After the pandemic, GHOS held quarterly meetings to oversee the implementation of the Basel III framework. 2017: GHOS endorsed the final framework of Basel III, which includes the revision of all frameworks, i.e, internal rating-based approach; operational risk; market risk; output floor; standardised approach for credit risk; and lastly, the leverage ratios. 2019: 100% implementation of the LCR framework 2019: GHOS endorsed revising the market-risk framework, which had been approved in 2017.	The Basel III framework had originally been postponed from January 2022 to January 2023 due to the pandemic. Jurisdictions have since adopted staggered timelines. **European Union (ex-UK):** Final implementation is set for January 2025 under the CRR III/CRD VI reforms. The EU Parliament approved the package in April 2024, with transitional arrangements until 2032. **United Kingdom:** The Prudential Regulation Authority (PRA) confirmed a phased rollout starting July 2025, with full compliance by January 2026. **United States:** The Federal Reserve proposed rules in October 2023 aligning with Basel III, targeting July 2025 for implementation. Final rules are pending as of Q1 2025. **Hong Kong:** Fully implemented Basel III as of January 2023. **Canada:** Adopted core Basel III standards in 2023, focusing on ongoing capital/liquidity enhancements. **Australia:** Major elements were implemented in 2023, with APRA prioritizing "unquestionably strong" capital buffers. **Japan:** Finalized Basel III adoption in March 2024 after a phased approach starting in 2021.

Source: own presentation, based on information from the financial regulatory authorities of the individual countries, and Bloomberg 'Fundamental Review Of The Trading Book (FRTB): Where Do We Stand?', Bloomberg.com, Last modified 2022 https://www.bloomberg.com/professional/blog/fundamentalreview-of-the-trading-book-frtb-where-do-we-stand/.

Risk Analysis Unit / Federal Reserve Bank of Atlanta
History of the Economy, Regulations & Bank Data
1782–Today

Event Type

Ⓐ Reporting
Ⓑ Data Provider
Ⓒ Recession/Depression
Ⓓ Bank Panic
Ⓔ Regulations
Ⓕ Examination
Ⓖ Banking Industry

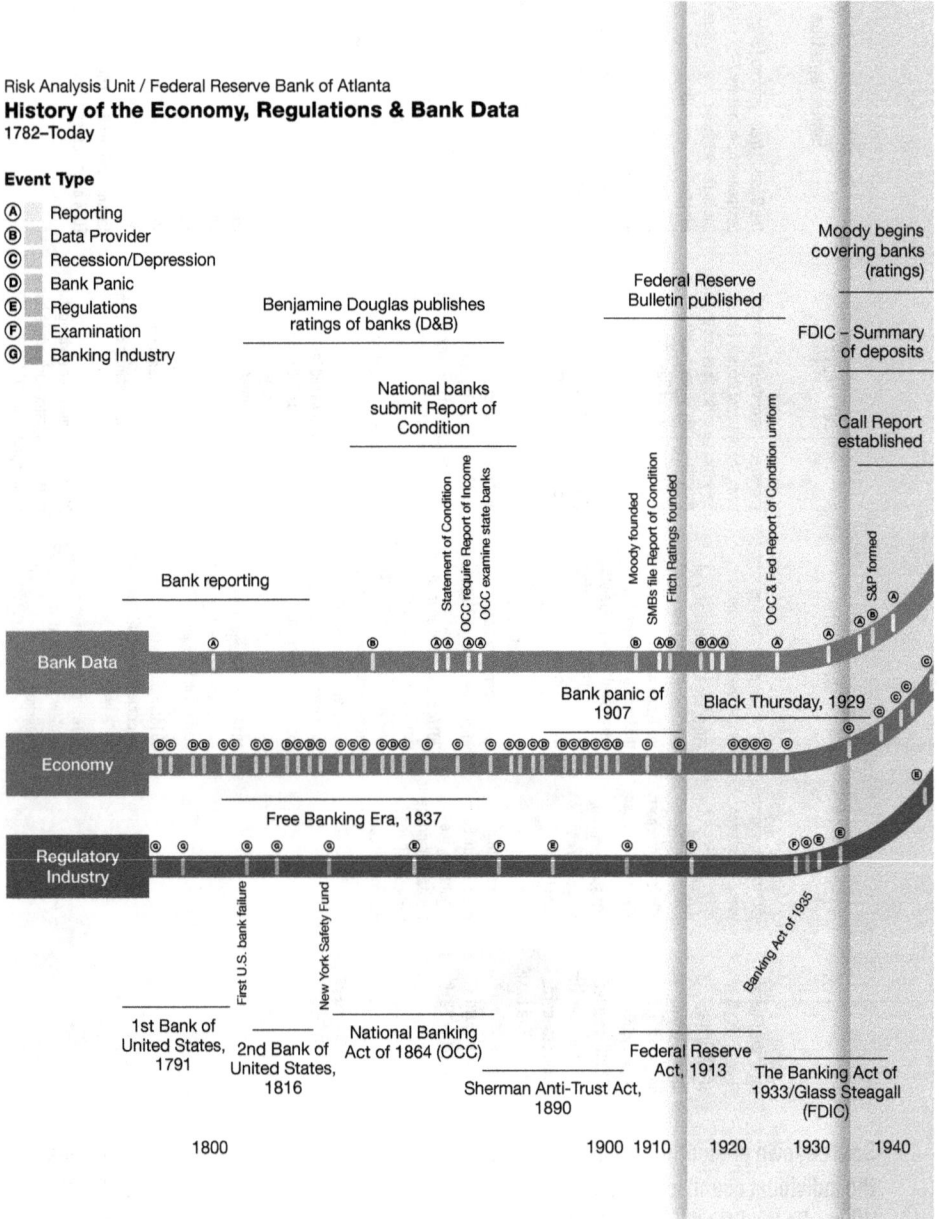

Moody begins
covering banks
(ratings)

Federal Reserve
Bulletin published

FDIC – Summary
of deposits

Benjamine Douglas publishes
ratings of banks (D&B)

National banks
submit Report of
Condition

Call Report
established

Statement of Condition
OCC require Report of Income
OCC examine state banks

Moody founded
SMBs file Report of Condition
Fitch Ratings founded

OCC & Fed Report of Condition uniform

S&P formed

Bank reporting

Bank Data

Bank panic of
1907

Black Thursday, 1929

Economy

Free Banking Era, 1837

**Regulatory
Industry**

First U.S. bank failure

New York Safety Fund

Banking Act of 1935

1st Bank of
United States,
1791

2nd Bank of
United States,
1816

National Banking
Act of 1864 (OCC)

Sherman Anti-Trust Act,
1890

Federal Reserve
Act, 1913

The Banking Act of
1933/Glass Steagall
(FDIC)

1800   1900 1910 1920   1930   1940

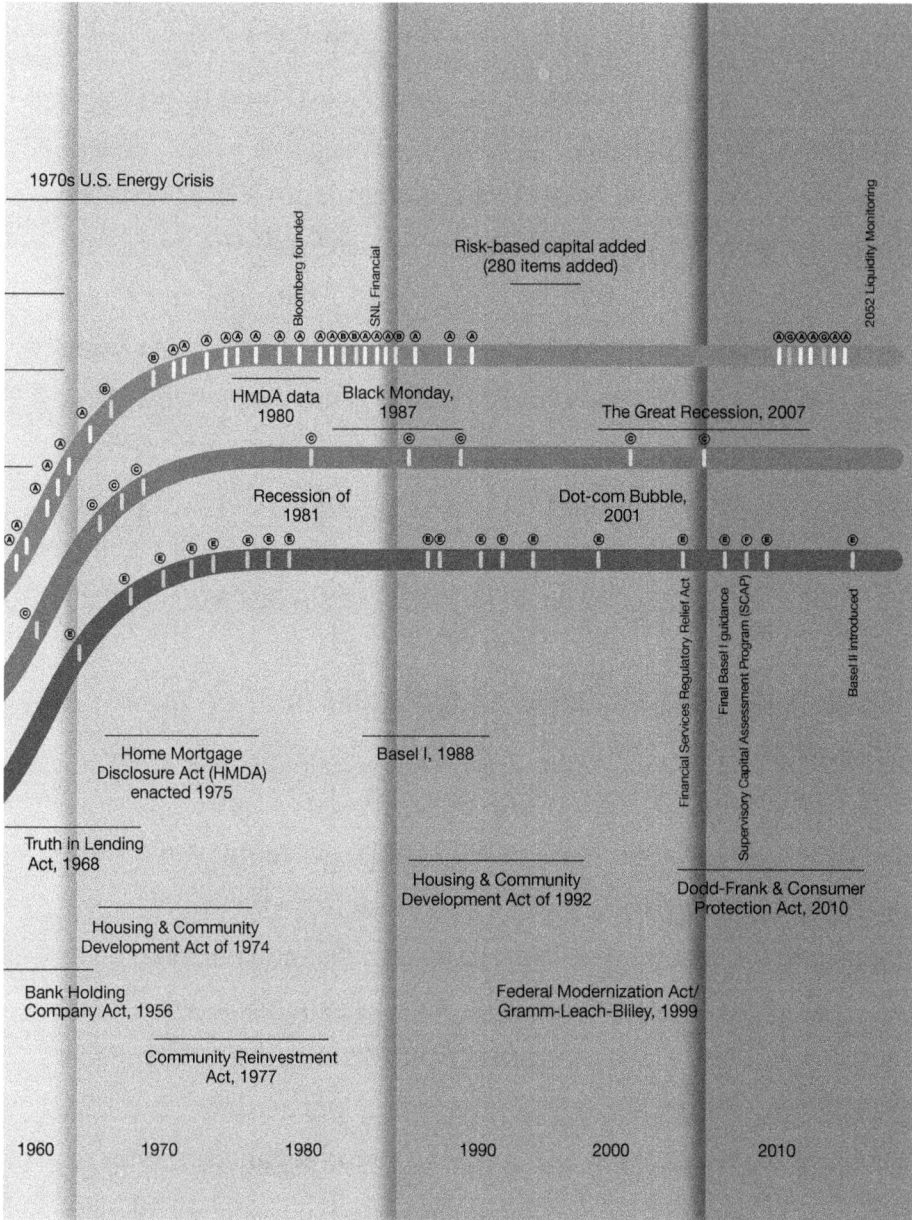

1970s U.S. Energy Crisis

Bloomberg founded

SNL Financial

Risk-based capital added
(280 items added)

2052 Liquidity Monitoring

HMDA data
1980

Black Monday,
1987

The Great Recession, 2007

Recession of
1981

Dot-com Bubble,
2001

Financial Services Regulatory Relief Act

Final Basel I guidance

Supervisory Capital Assessment Program (SCAP)

Basel II introduced

Home Mortgage
Disclosure Act (HMDA)
enacted 1975

Basel I, 1988

Truth in Lending
Act, 1968

Housing & Community
Development Act of 1992

Dodd-Frank & Consumer
Protection Act, 2010

Housing & Community
Development Act of 1974

Bank Holding
Company Act, 1956

Federal Modernization Act/
Gramm-Leach-Bliley, 1999

Community Reinvestment
Act, 1977

1960   1970   1980   1990   2000   2010

The above image illustrates the major government regulatory responses to a financial crisis in the history of the US economy. These regulations and laws were put in place to protect the market participants involved in a trade, a particular industry or sector specific regulations.

Such good intentions of preventive regulations have resulted in a multitude of unintended consequences for SMEs, primarily, making it harder for SMEs to access international trade and finance. To pick just one example, the number of banks providing trade credit in Africa between 2013 and 2019 has declined by 23 per cent. In short, large banks like to trade with large corporations. This is the SMEs' dilemma and an opportunity for companies like Artis and its investors.

Measures that trade financiers should take in their own interest

The core task for an internal or external legal team is to review each trade, to prepare and review transaction documentation, and to ensure compliance with national and international laws, restrictions and other guidelines such as sanctions, which can change over time. Clear transaction structuring and precise drafting is essential. At Artis, we are very particular about this.

At this point our trade is commercial and legally scrutinised. Once a trade is set in motion, various legal questions, not necessarily problems, will keep coming up, often around the quality and the delivery of the product.

If the debtor can prove that there is some sort of defect with the product or its quality – despite having approved the product already – it is the obligation of the factoring client, the borrower, to remedy the situation within a deadline. If the issue is not solved, the invoice is ceded back to the factoring party. Our legal team handles these transactions together with the credit insurer.

A simple example is one where a financing house realised that abiding by international regulations was only one part of the challenge. The investment firm did not realise that the country where they were looking to finance a trade had tariff minimums and stringent import laws.

The country where they intended to do business wouldn't allow the import of the merchandise in question and wouldn't allow cargo sizes as large as they had contractually agreed to provide. The result was a costly learning curve. The agency was forced to void the trade entirely.

Credit insurance

Trade credit insurance is typically taken out by exporters to mitigate the risk of non-payment by foreign buyers, whether due to insolvency, protracted default or political risk. However, trade financiers can also utilise this form of insurance. At Artis, we regularly use this instrument, ensuring that the insurance benefit is paid to the designated loss payee in the event of non-payment.

When talking about credit insurance, two terms need to be explained: the loss payee and the protected default clause. The loss payee is entitled to receive the claim payment in the event of a loss. International insurance regulations have significantly changed in recent years, particularly in trade credit insurance. Regulatory bodies like the International Association of Insurance Supervisors (IAIS) have introduced more stringent guidelines to enhance transparency and risk management. These reforms require insurers to adopt more robust frameworks for credit risk assessment and claims handling, especially in cross-border transactions. For example, new regulations emphasise the need for timely and accurate reporting of credit exposures, as well as more rigorous due diligence processes. These developments provide investors with increased protection and reliability, as insurers are now better equipped to manage and mitigate risks associated with international trade.

At Artis, our investment vehicles and managed account are the designated loss payees with our credit insurers, safeguarding investors from non-payment scenarios. Our arrangements include a protected default clause, ensuring that all claims are settled within six months, regardless of jurisdiction – a valuable safety net for investors seeking swift repayment in case of a buyer's default. Each deal (invoice) is insured, provided it meets specific criteria, such as adequate credit risk coverage.

Collateral covering

Even with legal mitigants and the appropriate protections in place, the risk of default or insolvency of the buyer remains. In addition to credit insurance, we might seek personal or corporate collateral covering the cost of funding the trade in question, where we only pay out after the product has been accepted by the buyer and the invoice raised. Failure to do so will lead to collection from the insurance company or on the collateral.

Artis's due diligence process and legal mitigation checklist

At Artis Trade Invest, we invest our own money to start with but also borrow funds from corporate and private lenders to gain more market share. In the following, you will understand the processes, how we deal with due diligence, trade-finance transactions, and most importantly, how we analyse the risks involved and how we mitigate them.

Before starting the Artis Trade Invest Program, my experiences in trade were many and varied, giving me a wide view of the trade-financing industry. Trade takes place and can be facilitated locally or around the world; it is somehow a product without borders but not without human hurdles. We had to dispel the myth that trade investment is only for the generationally wealthy or a class reserved for banks to finance from an investor perspective. Trade finance is a competitive and safe investment category and should be part of any balanced investment portfolio.

From a fund manager's perspective, investors should see trade finance as a profitable, secure asset class paying dividends predictably over the long term. Investment in trade is not speculative and has neither the ups nor downs of private equity, but rather the calm of a fixed-income type of investment.

In creating Artis, we wanted to combat the rigid modern-day structure of bank loans, to bring this affordable and lucrative investment option to the shareholders and SMEs who have the most to gain. Trade finance underpins trade at every stage of the supply chain. Peer-to-peer lending through trade finance is a modern form of investing. Trade finance provides an opportunity for investors to harvest yields with low risk and low volatility.

At Artis, we are committed to trade arrangements that benefit businesses, grow the world economy and create revenues for our shareholders. We study the markets, financial history and economic trends, to make trade finance available for eager investors regardless of their experience or expertise. We don't just move money around for stakeholders. We walk them through the process alongside project managers for an educational and transparent investing process.

Our contracts are thorough, written in line with local and international laws that pertain to each unique transaction. Though it sounds simple, structuring a trade-financing arrangement is a lengthy process.

We streamline the trading methodology and ensure that every trade works and satisfies all stakeholders' needs, including the firm, the investors and the importers and exporters involved.

Timeline of a typical trade transaction

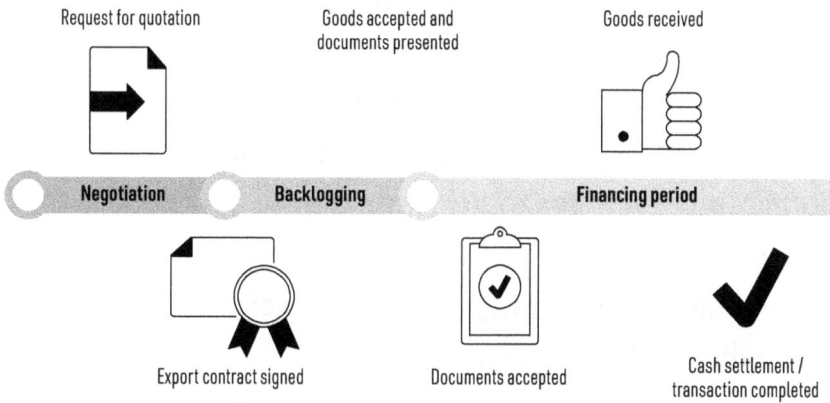

Request for quotation

Goods accepted and documents presented

Goods received

Negotiation   Backlogging   Financing period

Export contract signed

Documents accepted

Cash settlement / transaction completed

The typical process of a trade transaction

Next, we look at the layout of the Artis process for researching, structuring and assessing all trade deals and how a company complies with the sanctions imposed.

The process commences with the buyer's and seller's basic legal and financial background checks. We investigate the payment habits of our clients. Are there late payments, bankruptcies or pop-up, fly-by-night trading subsidiaries? Do the parties have a good relationship with their current distributors? What do average annual sales look like?

How much product can they produce/ship/move and so forth? In other words, we carry out in-depth desktop research combined with feedback from our networks, where available. The results are submitted to our risk-assessment team. We take a holistic approach to the business of our partners where credit assessment is important but not the only criterion.

An increasing number of investors expect the business or corporation to be committed to responsible investment. This is often a key consideration before investing. For investors today – and regardless of the size of investment – the social and environmental attitude of the investment target is not just another important box to tick; for many it has become a must. Responsible investing is encouraged by global trade regulators.

Let's take a step-by-step look at the checks we make to thoroughly analyse a trade.

Step 1: KYC (Know Your Customer) and AML (Anti-Money Laundering) – A necessary analysis

In the late sixties and into the seventies, there was a series on German TV, *Graf Yoster gibt sich die Ehre* ('Graf Yoster does the honours') and one of the episodes had the title: 'In London weiss der Nebel mehr als wir ...' ('In London, the fog knows more than we do'). It was similar to the British espionage television series *The Avengers*, and I have fond memories of it; it explains this section perfectly.

KYC serves as the guideline for preventing the abuse of the financial system with 'foggy' transactions, better known as AML – anti-money laundering. In theory, KYC can be pushed to endless degrees, so ideally common sense should be applied.

KYC and AML can present a real problem for companies trying to get legitimate payments completed promptly.

There seems to be no ceiling on what payment departments sometimes request in proof for payment. The latter is a real issue in today's working environment, where employees in the financial industry fear for their jobs if they make even small mistakes.

The identity-verification piece of KYC helps to prevent fraud in banking and to ensure that customers are who they claim to be. The process allows institutions to audit their customers and prevent them from committing fraud, tax evasion, financing terrorism and from committing other financial crimes the papers often write about.

Regulators want you to know your customer and your customer's customer's customer, and so on. A company must of course gather information on its customers to correctly identify them, monitor their transactions and assess the overall risk factors to mitigate them.

The KYC check includes AML requirements and consequently a focus on the importer-exporter relationship. International trade, especially since the digitalisation quantum leap, might invite those that shun the law to move funds derived from foggy trades, betting on a low risk of detection.

Money laundering happens all day long in many places that still function with cash such as coffee shops, laundrettes and other retailers. Mediterranean countries still use much more cash than the Nordic countries.

The first rule that flushes out most transgressions is always to request to speak to the party who writes the cheque or makes the transfer. This eliminates most people in the middle and transactions that exist only on paper evaporate.

AML covers the laws, regulations and procedures to shed light on the opaque. Technology has become a major driver for AML and KYC processes.

Absolute certainty is unrealistic. Those with 'foggy' intentions will not rely on standard payments systems to start with. Investigative journalism produced millions of documents in the 'Panama Papers' and the 'Paradise Papers' scandals, when millions of dollars' worth of 'dirty money' was exposed. Thorough due diligence along with a dose of common sense still goes a long way.

Today, even small companies, let alone multinationals, tend to spend considerable resources to comply with ever-increasing and often changing regulations. Compliance departments are still growing at a remarkable speed. The cost of doing trade has increased.

KYC and AML

- We check the reputation of the key stakeholder, management, board and shareholders.
- We check involved names against the Specially Designated Nationals List (SDN) and sanction list.

- We check the ultimate beneficial owners (UBO) of the companies involved, identifying who is/are the shareholder(s) and are shareholders a corporation, possibly owned by another company?
- When reviewing the banks involved on the buyer's and seller's side, we check the following:
  - Are these banks experienced in this type of transaction?
  - Are there any sanction issues?
  - Who are the shareholders of the bank, if it is not one of the known high-street names?

Step 2: Understanding the product

For trade financiers, validating a product goes far beyond regular inspections and testing. Artis takes time to fully understand the product being created, bought and sold as each shipment financed belongs to the company once an agreement is approved.

Artis's product inventory includes details of product(s) and components, where the manufactured items come from and where they are being sold to. We check whether supply-chain verification is possible and what collateral (LC, credit insurance or other) is in place.

To use an example, let us imagine that a flower shop in Zurich's prestigious Bahnhofstrasse receives fresh flowers from Ecuador, a major producer of cut flowers.

Regardless of the day of the week or the season, when the client enters the shop, the flowers must smell and look as fresh as if they had just been picked a few hours ago. Anything else is a loss for the shop owner. Selling 'end-of-the-day' flowers with a steep discount or not at all marks a bad end to the day. This example reminds us how the precision of process and logistics can decide between a successful trade or a financial loss.

At Artis, we decided not to get involved with perishable goods. Dried fruits, nuts and dates are the limit for us – fresh flowers or perishable goods including frozen fish are not a risk we wish to take at this point.

Understanding the product.

- We undertake a product check and analysis of the industry at large. Are products free of any sanctions? If not, which sanctions might apply (mainly US, EU, UN?) Lately, China and Russia entered the worldwide sanction 'competition', sanctioning mainly Western companies and individuals. These new national sanctions registers must now be monitored as well.
- We analyse possible dual use. This is especially important for raw materials and semi-finished products. Dual-use goods are items that can be used both for civilian and military applications. These types of goods are heavily regulated because they can be

classified for civilian use and then transformed for military purposes, or worse, used for terrorism.

- We check if the products are registered with a ministry, (usually health or industry), and if so, who is the registrar and responsible for the product's safe delivery in the country. If the products are not registered, we need to verify if registration is required and if any process has been initiated.

Step 3: Validating the counterparties: seller/buyer/importer/exporter

We focus on jurisdictions where we can rely on a reputable and experienced team on the ground and develop reliable business relationships across sectors and industries with sellers and buyers.

At the moment, our factoring focus is on Switzerland. However, we are exploring other hubs that fit our requirements and where there are strong teams on the ground, in particular Brazil, Germany and Greece.

We prefer repeat business and ongoing relationships with suppliers or exporters where we validate the process and rely on sellers' and buyers' proper execution. We verify the importers' market as well and its ability to sell the product. If the sale is unlikely, so is the repayment.

Once we validate the parties involved and the validity of the business concept, assessing the trade's economic sustainability comes next.

Validate counterparties.

- We check the seller's experience and reputation in their market, including previous trade volumes, frequencies of trades and financial volume per transaction and other types of experiences or problems.
- We investigate: Has the seller been affected by or has been subject to any US/UN/EU sanctions in the past?
- We validate ownership of the seller, especially if the business is privately owned. Listed companies are easier to verify.
- We analyse: How is the trade settled? (Ex-works, free on board, cost and freight or upon discharge?)
- We check payment terms. How is the payment cleared and through which party?

Step 4: Structuring the transaction

With the due diligence completed, it is time to structure the transaction to identify each party's role in the trade's financing. Risk mitigation remains key and the structure of the trade should satisfy all parties.

Flow of Funds

Flow of Goods

3. Manufacturer

2. Retailer

2. Retailer

4. Supplier

3. Manufacturer

1. Consumer

1. Consumer

4. Supplier

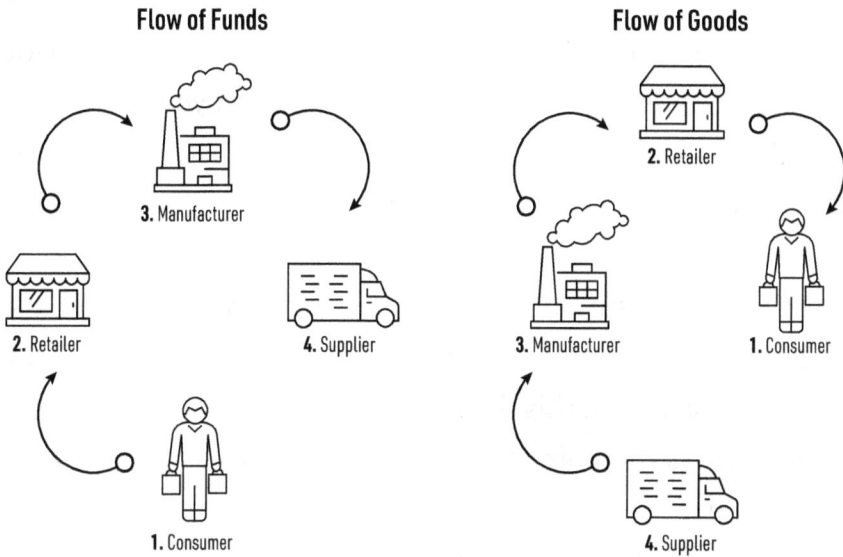

Open account refers to where the goods are shipped and delivered before the payment is due. While this is great for the buyer/importer, it can be a risk for the seller or exporter and can fall back on the financier in cases where the importer defaults or doesn't honour the agreed payment terms. Mobile or consumer goods cannot be recovered in case of non-payment as they have already been distributed. Open account trades are ideally credit insured. If a national export credit insurance policy does not cover the destination (some don't cover Sudan, for instance), personal or corporate guarantees might help.

Purchase and sale: here the financing party replaces the buyer and takes ownership of the asset financed. The financing party buys the export straight from the merchandiser, selling it to the importer, including the financing margin. This helps SMEs who require more flexible terms than an exporter can provide.

Where SMEs applying for trade financing have higher financial risks, catalytic credit-enhancement tools, like first-loss capital may be suitable. First-loss capital is defined by three features.

First, the investment firm will bear or cover the initial loss. The amount of loss covered is agreed upon upfront. In line with the risk taken, this financing tranche receives the highest return; this is the point at which hedge funds and speculators often invest.

Then, with the initial loss covered, the recipient's risk-return profile is improved, increasing the applicant's desirability for potential investors. Portfolio investors like this risk level. The third point is that it is a highly specific tool for a designated purpose.

Letters of Credit (LCs) are a bank's guarantee to pay the seller once the agreed-upon terms are fulfilled, ensuring the security of the transaction. They offer a secure mechanism for buyers and sellers to trade domestically and internationally, even when the parties have no prior business relationship.

The buyer's bank issues an LC, which serves as a legally binding promise to transfer payment to the exporter's bank on a specific future date, provided that the agreed-upon goods or services are exchanged under the specified terms. It is a modern counterpart to the banker's acceptance, discussed below.

An LC is generally irrevocable and contingent upon the submission of specific documents and adherence to set dates. It is a safeguard for the trade, giving both parties confidence that their shipments, payments, goods, services and deadlines will be respected.

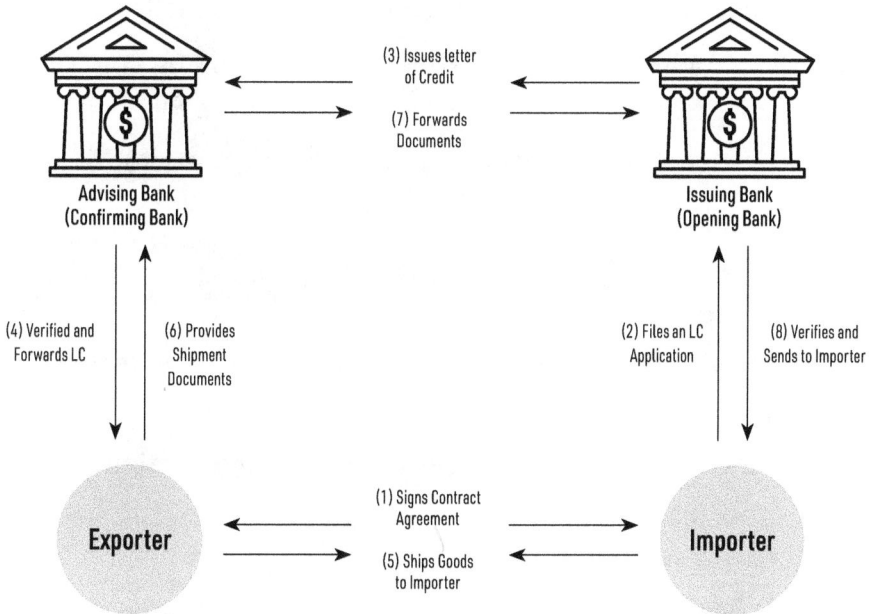

Advising Bank (Confirming Bank)

(3) Issues letter of Credit

(7) Forwards Documents

Issuing Bank (Opening Bank)

(4) Verified and Forwards LC

(6) Provides Shipment Documents

(2) Files an LC Application

(8) Verifies and Sends to Importer

Exporter

(1) Signs Contract Agreement

(5) Ships Goods to Importer

Importer

Ensuring that the transaction is sound and profitable before it reaches this point is vital. Once the documents are signed and the transaction has been launched, exporters and importers get to work securing the materials necessary and preparing to open their doors to customers.

Structuring the transaction.

When identifying the parties involved in the trade agreement, there are a few things to check:

- Is a financial or operational intermediary involved, or is it a direct sale?
- We look at the Companies House details of seller and buyer and details of intermediaries (if any) and create a diagram of the transactions, including the following:
    - names of all parties (direct, indirect, remote)
    - product flow(s)
    - money flow(s) and
    - contractual relationships.
- This all gives an immediate overview of the lie of the land and who is who in the transaction.
- We validate transaction design with an international exporter.
- Inform the importer.
- We check: Are there any other issues, whether related or unrelated?

Step 5: Risks identified

We have now covered the major areas of trade-financing risk, including political risks, supply-chain risk and, of course, the risk of human error among others. As much as trade-finance firms might love to support all SMEs, these various avenues of risk are all potential deal killers with new clients, even more so when working with international trades.

Whenever we look at a prospective client, Artis checks for certain business markers to start to get a sense of the new client. Any lack of validated financial records and related information is an initial warning sign and we might need to take a more holistic look at the business before moving forward with an agreement.

Companies that lack collateral pose yet another risk. If an SME is granted a financing agreement without putting forth collateral and ends up declaring bankruptcy or defaulting on its payments, the factoring company suffers the loss.

Depending on the transaction and the jurisdictions involved, collateral – personal or corporate – can be crucial for the outcome of an application; those who put forth substantial col-lateral are more likely to be approved for a financing agreement than the SME without it.

The KYC and AML laws and fintech companies have made a significant contribution to keeping trade safe but there is also the risk that KYC and AML laws will not catch all. We will cover KYC and AML more later, where we take an in-depth look at the risks associated with trade and trade financing.

Identify the risks.

- We undertake thorough risk mitigation on a micro to macro scale.
- We investigate each stakeholder and party involved, from an operational, transactional and reputational perspective.

Step 6: The deal process and sanctions

Once the deal is deemed commercially viable, the companies involved have been researched and validated and risks have been assessed and mitigated, the next stage is to process the deal. A trade deal has many moving parts.

It is essential that the deal structure is sound and that the relevant legal mitigants are applied, ensuring that all paperwork is in order. The transaction must follow the many national sanction regulations.

As an example, in late 2021 the US increased trade sanctions on Venezuela, prohibiting US companies and passport holders from trading with the country as well as prohibiting transactions with Venezuela in US dollars. Petrochemical transactions, including crude oil, became a particular focus.

An Asian company, for argument's sake, purchases agricultural goods from Venezuela or sells medical goods to Venezuela. The trade can be settled in either euros or Swiss francs. No sanctions of any kind are violated. The remaining problem is to find a bank willing to settle the trade, fearing for their banking relationship with the US, even though no sanction regime applies.

Sanctions are often a play of economic warfare thinly disguised in a legal framework, but in the end create the desired effect, preventing the sanctioned country from trading. It is a given that sanctions are intended to deter business with the sanctioned country. So how should even a seasoned entrepreneur best navigate the choppy waters of commercial sanctions?

A good beginning is to ask if any of the involved parties regardless of their size or importance, figure on any national or supranational sanctions list (EU/US/UN/Russia and China), and if so, to what degree? With this validation a knowledgeable decision can be made and an assessment made on whether a more in-depth KYC investigation is required. Involving resources like lawyers or investigation firms might be necessary to confirm the legality, often across various jurisdictions of the proposed transactions, or to start outlining the safe passage to transact in accordance with applicable sanction regulations.

In an ideal world, navigating international trade might be made easier if there were a single handbook with all the regulations one needs to know. Unfortunately, this does not exist. Each country or region, even cities (such as the Vatican) or international bodies (like the EU, UN, World Bank, International Monetary Fund, etc.) have their own different rules and regulations when it comes to trade.

These rules and regulations can come in the form of quotas, tariffs, non-tariff barriers, asset freeze/seizures or an embargo. Not all laws restrict trade outright, but every trade arrangement needs to meet the different thresholds depending on where the transaction is being executed and who the importers and exporters are, as well as the state of international trade itself.

Quotas are government-imposed trade regulations that limit trade in some form. Sometimes the number of items shipped can be limited, or goods of a particular monetary value can't be sent at any time; or the government will restrict how much can be sold in any given period, which would also be considered a quota.

When any asset like land or property owned by an importer or exporter can be essentially frozen, this means that the owned property can't be moved or sold unless it's done by or with the approval of the sanctioning nation. International laws remain vague about these matters.

Quotas and asset freezes are tools used by governments to stop or limit trade with individuals, companies or economies.

Tariffs are mostly known as import taxes collected by the government. They fluctuate depending on the ever-changing political climate. Non-tariff barriers are restrictions on imported goods unrelated to taxes like specific licensing requirements or product standards. These are another tool for encouraging or discouraging trades of goods or services and financing arrangements. While tariffs don't fully deter trade, they create costs and affect the overall financial result.

Finally, we have embargos. An embargo is the most limiting of all the legal sanctions, most commonly a complete ban on trade. This can be a ban on commercial activity in general, but sometimes it is just on the trade itself. Being up to date on embargos and where they exist is of the utmost importance for successfully navigating trade deals internationally.

We check each transaction, product and person against the current sanctions list. The process is cumbersome, extensive and unavoidable. It is the only safe way to operate within the safe sanction 'corridor' and our clients appreciate having support from our in-house legal and risk team.

An offence against sanction laws is far from trivial and is considered a criminal offence by many jurisdictions, especially the US. A good criminal (not commercial) lawyer or barrister can offer valuable advice to SMEs who wish to engage with countries featuring on some countries' sanction list and can be an excellent last source of guidance prior to signing a transaction.

Over all our years in the trade business, we have avoided legal problems. This is in no small part thanks to this lengthy due diligence, common sense and our dedicated and innovative team. Be stringent about whom you deal with. Make mistakes in the process and a whole deal can end up going sour, or an entire production line can be stopped short if a just-in-time product shipment is late. The last few years have demonstrated the supply issues being experienced around the globe.

Trade finance offers an abundance of opportunities. It is the job of Artis to navigate our partners through this economic

'Bermuda Triangle' safely. Good processes keep matters straight.

We manage reputational and payment worries for our clients. On the advisory side, we sell aspirin for trade 'headaches', so to speak. For example, in 2020 and 2021 we helped European companies who did not wish to send their team members to Kabul in person, regarding their tenders with the Afghan government of that time. We act for companies in a variety of sectors, from paint and insurance to pharmaceuticals and tractors.

When Artis is not working as an agent for a client, then we are helping companies to finance their imports or open bank accounts. A bread-and-butter case is to facilitate acceptance of LCs or monetise credit lines through Trade Repo agreements. Quite a few SMEs find it difficult to get their LC confirmed.

As covered previously, LCs cannot be issued in non-convertible currencies. We can often accept local or non-confirmed LCs. With businesses in the UK, the EU, Switzerland, the Middle East and Central Asia, we provide the counterparty that suits the trade, in the correct currency and right jurisdiction.

In the face of new technology, we have streamlined our workflow and digitised many of our processes for increased efficiency, shorter application processing times and early fraud detection (of LCs, mainly). Fintech's combination of blockchain and AI came as a blessing and has drastically changed the trade-financing landscape. It will continue to enable increased clarity, profitability and efficiency in the future of this trade sector.

Awareness: Only transparency can create trust

One of humanity's most remarkable traits is our capacity for awareness. As we approach the mid 2020s and beyond, the trade finance industry is set for significant transformation driven by several emerging trends. Digital innovation continues to gain momentum, with advancements in AI and blockchain technologies enhancing the efficiency and security of trade finance operations. The rise of virtual currencies and decentralised finance (DeFi) platforms is expected to revolutionise international trade payments, offering faster, more secure and cost-effective cross-border transactions.

Another significant trend shaping the trade finance landscape is the integration of ESG factors. This is not just a trend, but a fundamental shift that is increasingly essential. Financial institutions are now incorporating ESG criteria into their decision-making processes, leading to the development of sustainability-linked trade finance products such as green bonds and ESG-linked loans. This shift not only supports global sustainability goals but also creates attractive opportunities for investors looking to align their portfolios with ethical and sustainable practices.

Transparency is the key to building trust in trade finance. Only when processes are transparent and easily understood will trade finance gain wider acceptance among private investors and become recognised as a valuable asset class. This is why we developed our six-step framework for processing trades, which minimises risk for all parties involved, including investors and trade partners. As outlined above, the framework addresses critical areas such as legal compliance, fraud risk and domestic or cross-border sanctions, guiding investors toward enhanced returns. These are all factors that investors consider critical when selecting their investments.

Chapter 7:

Environmental, Social and Governance Criteria: Sustainability in Trade

As previously mentioned, sustainability is becoming increasingly crucial in international trade and it also applies to trade financing. John Denton, Secretary-General of the International Chamber of Commerce, has emphasised the importance of sustainable practices, stating, 'Not only do global supply chains account for up to 80 per cent of the economy's carbon emissions, but they are responsible for the work and livelihoods of billions of people. As such, parties involved must conduct business in a way that protects our planet and the people who live on it.'

At the 2024 ESG XChange Summit, global leaders underscored the growing urgency of robust ESG practices to combat climate change, stressing that sustainable strategies in global supply chains are essential to achieving environmental goals while safeguarding billions of livelihoods. A critical statement from the Summit highlighted, 'The intersection of sustainability and trade is no longer optional but necessary to address the pressing climate crisis and its widespread impact on global economies.'

At Artis, we are fully committed to incorporating ESG into trade finance. This approach enables us to achieve strong investment returns and fosters credibility and responsibility in the industry.

This chapter delves into ESG's specific implications for trade finance. Environmental, social and governance criteria have become the cornerstone of responsible investing for institutions worldwide. We will explore how trade finance can enhance a company's financial position and improve its ESG performance.

Governments and consumers are becoming more conscious of sustainability issues in trade, manufacturing and retail. This has led to mounting pressure on all participants in the value chain – manufacturers, financial institutions, logistics providers, distributors and retailers. Sustainability has become a central issue in policymaking, increasing the demand for transparency across manufacturing and supply chains.

The digitisation of trade finance contributes significantly to environmental sustainability while making trade more accessible for emerging markets and businesses. By integrating blockchain and other digital tools, trade finance is becoming more efficient, reducing costs and environmental impact and paving the way for a more sustainable and inclusive global trade ecosystem.

Making trade greener

As global trade transitions from traditional cash transactions to digital ecosystems, the trade finance industry is transforming profoundly, shedding its reliance on outdated paper-based processes. This shift is propelled by legal and regulatory reforms that now facilitate the exchange of digital trade documents and data. Countries such as the UAE, Singapore and the UK have taken the lead in these efforts, with landmark initiatives like the Model Law on Electronic Transferable Records (MLETR) and the UK's Electronic Trade Documents Act of 2023, setting new standards for digital trade.

This transformation modernises trade finance and plays a pivotal role in making global trade greener. The reduced environmental footprint, combined with increased accessibility for SMEs worldwide, underscores how digital advancements shape a more sustainable and inclusive future for international commerce. These innovations are not just trends; they are necessary evolutions that address the urgent need for responsible and innovative trade practices in the face of climate change.

Additionally, suppliers who meet specific environmental performance goals can now access more favourable interest rates, driving positive change across industries.

While the future of ESG does not rest solely on trade finance, the industry plays a critical role in facilitating the achievement of sustainability goals. As Duncan Lodge, Global Head of Traditional Trade at Bank of America, put it: 'One of the interesting things about trade finance is that normally something has to happen before someone gets paid – presenting a document under a letter of credit or onboarding a supplier into a supply chain finance program – so it provides a set of natural controls. While we have specific ESG solutions, traditional trade finance can be used as-is to support ESG activities across the board.'

From letters of credit used to procure wood pellets for biomass plants to performance guarantees for export credit agency-backed wind farm projects, ESG has become a crucial component of any trade finance business model.

Trade finance drives the implementation of ESG

Trade finance has both a direct and an indirect influence on the real economy. When trade-finance providers such as merchant companies and banks build personal relationships in key commodity markets, it provides invaluable insight and market intelligence, which in turn leads to better lending decisions. This creates better returns and fewer losses for underlying investors.

These business relationships allow lenders to connect with SMEs directly, promoting ESG principles in trade finance through active engagement. Asia and Africa employ the highest usage of trade finance and, consequently, account for the highest priority regarding ESG development, being in a prime position to meet the UN sustainability development goals of promoting corporate governance and transparency; eradicating child and slave labour; and eliminating discrimination.

Shaping a sustainable future

As businesses increasingly prioritise sustainability, global trade finance must evolve to meet the demands of environmental, social and governance criteria. ESG-driven trade finance goes beyond facilitating transactions. It contributes to sustainable development by directing investments toward positive environmental and social impact projects.

Some multinational financial institutions facilitate substantial ESG-compatible financing and investments, with meaningful percentages directed toward green and sustainable activities. By financing projects that enhance energy efficiency, reduce waste and promote renewable energy use, trade finance can contribute to environmental sustainability while potentially delivering robust financial returns.

Moreover, the social impact of trade finance is plentiful. Closing the trade finance gap helps reduce poverty, enabling more businesses – especially in low-income countries – to participate in global trade, creating more jobs and improving access to essential goods. This impact is particularly vital for small and women-led businesses disproportionately affected by the trade finance gap. Trade finance fosters more inclusive and equitable economies, supporting these enterprises and contributing to global social and economic development.

A few examples

In April 2019 HSBC and Walmart jointly rolled out a sustainable supply-chain finance programme, pegging a supplier's financing rate to its performance against sustainability targets. Rabobank has set specific ESG key performance indicators (KPIs) for its borrowers. These KPIs are verified every year and, if on target, the borrower will benefit from a reduced financing rate subsidised by the borrowers that do not meet the KPIs and are charged higher financing rates.

In the 2021 report on financing for sustainable development, the UN has made it clear that it is crucial to bridge the trade-finance gaps that greatly influence SMEs and hinder exporters from acquiring trade opportunities. The equality progress sustainability bond (EPSB), where linked with better ESG performance in companies' supply chains, optimises funding by reducing costs.

Corporate and private investors and business managers need to know how to benefit from ESG in trade, to put it to work and allocate resources better along with other asset classes. To make this happen, it is essential that an ESG strategy is implemented and executed appropriately.

Trade finance as an asset class was for a long time beyond reach, at least for the general investor relying on their banker's recommendation, but the demand for capital has increased in the goods and services industry and banks are not willing to increase their exposure to funding this new demand – indeed, under the

Basel agreements, they are not allowed to. A strong team is critical and able to build valuable partnerships across industries and networks gaining valuable insight from the market.

Case study: Cocoa from Ghana

How does trade finance add value to society and business? A case study might provide some answers. Ghana and Ivory Coast are worldwide leaders in cocoa production and in countries like this, the small farmers working on these crops are highly skilled in anything relating to the crop but often lack business connections and strong networks. Trade finance boosts productivity and output levels.

The Touton company has been operational in Ivory Coast and Ghana for over 25 years. For eight of these years, it has worked with Eurofin Asia Group Pte. Ltd (EFA), a Singapore-based independent asset manager specialising in private-debt strategies to gain capital and finance. Touton uses EFA's services to provide better opportunities for the small-scale farmers that work the cocoa fields in Ghana. They have also launched impressive programmes such as the 2008 Ghana sustainability programme and a farm development approach plan to help the small farmers achieve their goals.

Touton's impact from these initiatives has been remarkable, helping almost 80,000 farmers across the two countries. The farmers are taught business skills and their attention is directed towards the ideas of land rehabilitation and crop diversification. These concepts both treat the land as a sacred resource, preventing overuse and assuring diversification in cash crops (a readily saleable crop that is grown and gathered for the market such as vegetables, cotton or tobacco).

Putting in so much effort to develop sustainable relationships with their farmers yields better results and creates more jobs for the community. It also helps the farmers learn valuable skills.

In several areas, trade finance has improved the general business environment and brought about a higher level of sustainability. It has equipped local producers with better skills and more income opportunities. The changing dynamics of the markets, industrial and financial, suggest that the demand for such trade-financing practices will only increase in the future.

Support from multilateral institutions

Support from major financial institutions is crucial in driving the global adoption of factoring as a reliable trade finance tool. For example, the European Bank for Reconstruction and Development's Legal Transition Programme has focused on improving legal frameworks for factoring, with specific emphasis on promoting the UNIDROIT Model Law on Factoring.

The widespread adoption of factoring laws is expected to positively impact international trade and global markets by providing businesses with more accessible and reliable financing options, thereby promoting greater participation in global supply chains. Sadly, regional and international regulations often put a spanner into such attempts at market participation.

What's ahead?

The global green finance market is projected to grow from $4.18 trillion in 2023 to $28.7 trillion by 2033, underscoring the rising significance of sustainability in finance. Trade finance is set to play a pivotal role in this transformation.

The focus on ESG in trade finance is expected to intensify, driven by regulatory pressures and growing investor demand for sustainable practices. One key trend is the increasing emphasis on transparency and responsible sourcing. Companies must increasingly demonstrate that their supply chains are free from environmental harm, human rights abuses, and other unethical practices. This shift will likely be accompanied by stricter reporting standards, requiring more detailed disclosures on ESG performance.

Another major trend is the rise of impact investing within trade finance, where investors actively seek opportunities that deliver both financial returns and positive social or environmental outcomes. This approach reshapes investment strategies and encourages companies to innovate and adopt more sustainable business models.

By aligning with ESG principles, trade finance supports individual companies and contributes to the development of a more sustainable and resilient global economy.

Chapter 8:

Recent Developments: Decentralised Finance and Blockchain in Trade Finance

The world is changing fast and trade finance is no exception. Indeed, the statements in this chapter may quickly become outdated due to the rapid developments in the sector. Recent innovations have significantly transformed how business is conducted, with decentralised finance (DeFi) emerging as a revolutionary force powered by blockchain technology. Let's delve into how these developments are reshaping the trade finance landscape.

Over the past few years, DeFi has revolutionised the industry, bringing unprecedented transparency, efficiency and accessibility through blockchain technology and smart contracts. These innovations are opening new doors for investors and reshaping global trade finance. This chapter highlights the key developments shaping the sector's future.

One of blockchain's most powerful features is its ability to enable unrelated parties to conduct transactions and share data transparently on a shared ledger. This technology allows various components of a trade – documents, payments and logistics – to function synergistically rather than sequentially, streamlining the entire process.

The old trade-financing system involved significant delays as each step required completion before advancing to the next stage, often stalling the entire process while documents were reviewed and passed along. With fintech's integration of blockchain technology, these bottlenecks have been eliminated. Transactions are now encrypted, secure and, most importantly, transparent. The need for third-party intermediaries to verify and facilitate transactions has become obsolete, making the system more efficient.

The future of trade finance is centred around fintech solutions that streamline due diligence and financing arrangements. With blockchain, financing agreements can be automatically shared with relevant banks through smart contracts. This reduces what was once a two-week process to a single step: pressing a button. In real time, an importer's bank can review purchase agreements, draft credit terms and submit the payment obligation to the exporter's bank, all within the blockchain ecosystem.

Export banks can immediately review and approve payment obligations. Once approved, smart contracts are generated on the blockchain. The exporter signs the blockchain equivalent of a letter of credit (LC), initiating the smart contract and automatically scheduling the first shipment.

The efficiency extends to customs inspections as well. Using blockchain, third-party customs agents at both exporting and importing ports can access the same digital documents, eliminating the need for multiple sets of paperwork. Upon delivery, the importer reviews the goods and, if satisfied, signs off via blockchain, triggering the automatic release of payment.

This enhanced transparency also benefits international regulators. Real-time snapshots of essential documentation allow regulators to monitor compliance, enforce international regulations and detect potential fraud. Traders, financiers and regulators no longer need to rely on manual updates – they are automatically notified via blockchain as each step is completed.

The process of disintermediation – removing the middleman from the equation – also benefits banks involved in issuing LCs. With updated technology, banks no longer need to assume risk. Instead, the risk transfers to the investing firm, such as Artis, or the supporting credit insurer.

At Artis, our risk-mitigation strategy is firmly embedded in practice. Blockchain-based contracts help reduce counterparty risk by enabling investors to access bills of lading – legal documents issued by carriers detailing the goods being shipped. A bill of lading certifies that specific cargo has already been financed and is en route to its destination. This digital approach eliminates the risk of double spending or double financing, a common concern in the trade finance industry and significantly reduces the potential for fraud.

The most compelling feature of this technology is its automated settlement capability, which reduces transaction fees. With a simple click and digital signature upon delivery of goods, payment is automatically processed to the exporter. This not only eliminates unnecessary paperwork but also reduces transaction costs.

Fintech has provided Artis with significant opportunities for growth. The trade finance sector is evolving and those embracing fintech stand to benefit the most.

Transforming trade finance with decentralised finance: A new era for investors

Decentralised finance lending platforms extend beyond high-risk, high-return paradigms and redefine accessibility and efficiency in global trade. DeFi platforms are poised to reshape trade finance by lowering barriers to entry for a broader range of investors while enhancing transparency. Let's take a closer look at how they do that and what challenges they present.

Decentralised finance lending versus traditional lending

Both DeFi lending and traditional lending facilitate international access to diverse investment opportunities, but their similarities end there.

DeFi lending involves peer-to-peer lending using crypto assets, which offers the potential for high returns by appreciating the underlying token with various degrees of volatility. Traditional lending uses fiat currencies, such as USD, GBP and JPY. Most

DeFi lending contracts are substantially more complex and longer, requiring particular legal knowledge in the crypto sphere and additional scrutiny and structuring.

DeFi lending attracts investors seeking higher yields. The underlying crypto risk is directly linked to the coin or token. Stablecoins are connected to the volatility of the underlying currency. In contrast, other crypto assets might have higher volatility. Traditional asset-backed lending suits institutional investors, mid-market enterprises and individuals seeking stable, uncorrelated and short-duration yields.

Lastly, DeFi lending varies based on national crypto regulations, potentially complicating investments when transferring from a crypto platform or exchange to traditional banks. Fiat-based asset-backed lending in trade finance ensures compliance with established regulatory frameworks, maintaining investor trust and legal adherence.

The benefits of decentralised finance in trade finance

DeFi offers a whole range of advantages in trade finance. Let's summarise them:

- **Lower entry barriers:** Investing in trade finance demands significant capital, which often limits access to institutional or professional investors. DeFi platforms democratise access by accepting smaller amounts, allowing more participants to invest. For example, regulated alternative investment funds give access only to qualified or professional investors and the minimum investment is commonly in the six figures. Regulated DeFi platforms allow investors to onboard with as little as $100 through DeFi's specific investment pool, dramatically broadening participation opportunities. While capital requirements are lower, investing through these platforms requires some technical affinity and familiarity with wallets. You must formally onboard with your ID on a regulated DeFi platform and then link your wallet to invest.

- **Enhanced transparency:** Traditional trade finance transactions often lack real-time transparency. Blockchain technology, which the DeFi world relies on, improves transparency and ensures visibility into transactions and borrower creditworthiness. Investors can access immutable records on the blockchain, which provides a more transparent, more up-to-date view of financial health and transaction history.

- **Efficient investment processes:** Smart contracts automate and expedite operations, which speeds settlement times and reduces operational costs by eliminating intermediaries. This creates more seamless transactions. DeFi platforms enhance investment efficiency by enabling global transfers at any time.

- **Global reach:** Smaller trade finance operators, including us, often focus on specialty sectors or regions where they have particular know-how and avoid complex cross-border transactions. The evolving and diverse regulatory frameworks across jurisdictions require investors to be cautious, highlighting the need for awareness of opportunities and risks, including the DeFi sector.

- **Improved credit risk management:** DeFi platforms like to mitigate credit risk through over-collateralisation, where borrowers must provide collateral that exceeds the loan amount. For instance, if a trade finance fund borrows $100,000 from a DeFi platform, it may need to secure the loan with $130,000 worth of real-world assets. This approach reduces the lender's exposure to market volatility and enhances security for investors.

The risks and challenges of decentralised finance in trade finance

While DeFi platforms offer advantages for trade finance, they also present challenges and risks investors are encouraged to consider:

- **Regulatory uncertainty:** DeFi regulations are still evolving. The lack of uniform global regulations can complicate investments, as platforms might need to comply with diverse legal requirements, potentially affecting their stability and legality.
- **Specialised knowledge requirements:** Investors often need specialised knowledge to navigate the DeFi space effectively. Before engaging, understanding blockchain

technology, smart contracts and the specific mechanics of DeFi platforms is recommended. This can limit accessibility for less technology-patient investors accustomed to a more analogue approach.

- **Market volatility and liquidity issues:** While over-collateralisation mitigates risk, volatility resides in the value of cryptocurrencies, even stablecoins that are pegged to the market value of an underlying currency such as USDT, a USD-pegged stablecoin.
- **Operational and security risks:** The technology underpinning DeFi is still relatively new and can be prone to operational issues and security vulnerabilities. Smart contract bugs and platform exploits can lead to significant losses for investors if not adequately addressed. Investors should do their due diligence about the DeFi counterparty, some of which enjoy an excellent track record.

Decentralised finance platforms might help to narrow the trade finance gap

DeFi platforms showcase blockchain technology's power to provide secure, transparent and efficient financial services and money transfers for trade finance.

By using alternative data sources such as transaction histories and digital footprints instead of traditional credit scores, DeFi platforms enable a broader spectrum of businesses to qualify for financing, especially in smaller markets. This inclusive strategy impacts economic growth and development.

By tokenising trade receivables or other assets, DeFi platforms enhance liquidity and widen the pool of potential investors. This development helps democratise access to trade finance, allowing investors with smaller capital to participate.

Finally, DeFi is poised to narrow the estimated $2.6 trillion trade finance gap more swiftly than traditional methods could. Its internet-native framework streamlines processes and eliminates long-standing barriers, marking a significant milestone where digitalisation surpasses conventional financial models. Embracing DeFi could herald a new era where better financial inclusion and technological innovation converge, profoundly reshaping global trade dynamics.

Chapter 9:

Artis's Growing Business Space: Exploring Trade in Saudi Arabia

In 2017 Saudi Crown Prince Mohammed bin Salman declared his bold vision that 'The Middle East will be the new Europe', setting the tone for the country's grand Vision 2030. This comprehensive initiative aims to diversify Saudi Arabia's economy, reduce its dependence on oil and transform the Kingdom into a global investment centre. Trade finance is at the heart of this transformation, a vital pillar supporting Saudi Arabia's emergence as an economic leader regionally and globally.

Central to Vision 2030 is the Kingdom's effort to create a more sustainable and diversified economy that attracts foreign direct investment and fosters private-sector growth. This shift from an oil-centric economy to sectors such as manufacturing, logistics, technology and renewable energy requires an efficient financial system where trade finance plays a fundamental role as it provides the liquidity, risk mitigation and economic mechanisms that support cross-border trade and investment, allowing businesses to operate smoothly in international markets.

Trade Works

Trade finance in Saudi Arabia has not only fuelled growth in non-oil exports. It paved the way for global trade corridors, bolstering the Kingdom's position in international trade. As the largest economy of the Gulf Cooperation Council (GCC), Saudi Arabia's focus on technological innovation and financial reforms lays the groundwork for a more resilient, interconnected economy, with trade finance as the mainstay.

Saudi Arabia's economic powerhouse strategy

KSA plays a pivotal role in shaping the region's economic landscape. In 2023 Saudi Arabia's GDP stood at nearly $1 trillion, contributing almost 30 per cent of the GCC's combined imports and exports. This economic dominance is underpinned by the Kingdom's vast natural resources, strategic location and forward-looking investment policies. Trade finance facilitates the seamless movement of goods and capital across borders, ensuring liquidity and significantly reducing the risks associated with global trade, thus contributing to the stability of the Saudi economy.

Saudi Arabia's robust trade finance ecosystem has provided the infrastructure necessary to sustain cross-border trade flows, crucial for supporting the economy's diversification. The Saudi Export Program (SEP) offers financing solutions to exporters, ensuring they can compete in international markets while minimising risks related to foreign exchange fluctuations and payment delays. These initiatives allowed Saudi businesses to integrate more deeply into global value chains, with trade finance as the essential enabler.

Diversifying beyond oil

For decades, Saudi Arabia's economy relied heavily on oil exports, accounting for over 70 per cent of government revenue. Sectors like new manufacturing, tourism, logistics and renewable energy are crucial for reducing the economy's vulnerability to oil price fluctuations and creating a more sustainable, diversified economic base.

The high-tech manufacturing sector, a key growth area under Vision 2030, relies heavily on sophisticated trade finance products such as factoring, letters of credit, supply chain financing and export credit insurance. These instruments help manufacturers secure materials, manage payment risks and ensure timely delivery of goods across borders, facilitating seamless trade.

The rise of renewable energy projects – such as solar and wind farms and the production of green hydrogen – has been driven by project finance and green trade finance projects helping Saudi Arabia's shift towards a more sustainable energy mix. Saudi Arabia's commitment to sustainability is evident in its investment in green projects such as Neom, a $500 billion smart city that aims to be a global leader in sustainable living. Trade finance's role in developing these projects cannot be overstated, providing the necessary capital to fund construction, supply chains and technology imports. The Kingdom's Green Initiative, launched in 2021, further emphasises the role of sustainability in shaping Saudi Arabia's economic future. Trade finance will be instrumental in financing these initiatives, mainly through green bonds and sustainable finance products.

The logistics sector, critical for Saudi Arabia's goal of being a global hub for transport and trade, has benefited from targeted investments supported by trade finance. Saudi Arabia's expanding logistics and infrastructure sectors, supported by strategic projects like Neom and the Red Sea Project, are expected to boost non-oil exports significantly. These mega projects will position the Kingdom as a global hub for trade, enhancing its export capabilities by connecting it to major global trade routes. Developing world-class infrastructure, like ports and airports, is vital in improving the Kingdom's connectivity to international trade routes, further enabling the flow of goods and services into and out of Saudi Arabia.

Growth projections

Saudi Arabia's non-oil exports are projected to grow at a compound annual growth rate (CAGR) of 13 per cent through 2030, with total exports expected to reach $354 billion by the same year. This impressive growth trajectory directly results from the Kingdom's determined efforts to diversify its economy.

Investments in digital trade finance technologies, including blockchain and AI-powered platforms, further drive this growth.

These technologies are transforming how trade finance is conducted, providing faster and more transparent processes, which are especially valuable for Saudi companies looking to expand their presence in global markets. This is a crucial development as the Kingdom ramps up its high-tech goods and services exports, sectors that require agile, efficient financing solutions.

The role of trade finance in Vision 2030

A commitment to economic diversity is at the core of Saudi Arabia's Vision 2030. Vision 2030 outlines several core objectives, including expanding the role of the private sector, increasing foreign direct investment (FDI) and boosting non-oil exports.

A primary goal of Vision 2030 is to cultivate a robust private sector, aiming for it to contribute 65 per cent of the GDP. Trade finance is a natural, critical enabler, empowering private-sector companies to venture into new markets and compete globally. With solutions like supply chain finance, export credit insurance and trade receivables financing, Saudi companies can secure working capital and manage payment risks, facilitating their international expansion.

Another driver of Vision 2030 is the increase in foreign direct investment, which will make Saudi Arabia an attractive hub for international businesses. In this context, trade finance creates a more stable and predictable investment environment, reducing cross-border transaction risks. This reassurance encourages foreign companies to establish operations in Saudi Arabia.

Saudi Arabia accelerates its exports in sectors including automotive manufacturing, pharmaceuticals and agriculture, with trade finance providing the tools to manage the risks of entering new, often volatile, international markets.

The rise of SMEs

SMEs are the backbone of Saudi Arabia's economic development and diversification efforts. Across the MENA (Middle East and Northern Africa) region, SMEs account for the vast majority of businesses and employ a significant portion of the labour force, with estimates suggesting they comprise up to 97 per cent of businesses and employ nearly 50 per cent of workers in some countries. In Saudi Arabia, the government is committed to increasing the contribution of SMEs to GDP from 20 per cent to 35 per cent by 2030, recognising the sector's potential as a driver of innovation and job creation.

Government initiatives such as Monsha'at's Funding Gate (Tamweel) have delivered impressive results, facilitating an 884 per cent increase in SME borrowing year-on-year and supporting over 2,770 enterprises. These initiatives have also significantly reduced service delivery times, from an average of 86 days in 2020 to just 7 days in 2021. Despite these improvements, the MENA region continues to face a $123 billion financing gap, underscoring the significant opportunities for trade finance solutions to address this regional challenge.

This is where emerging technologies like Banking as a Service (BaaS) and Lending as a Service (LaaS) come into play. Globally, BaaS is projected to generate a market opportunity worth $7 trillion by 2030, presenting significant potential for adoption in Saudi Arabia as part of its SME financing strategy. LaaS enables SMEs to integrate financing requests into existing ERP (Enterprise Resource Planning) systems, significantly accelerating lending processes and reducing delays compared to traditional methods.

The emergence of non-banking players

In recent years Saudi Arabia has witnessed a surge of non-banking financial players transforming the trade finance landscape and empowering SMEs. These players, including peer-to-peer lending platforms, crowdfunding platforms and private debt providers, offer innovative solutions to address the financing gap SMEs face. By circumventing traditional banking institutions, these platforms give businesses faster access to capital, helping them secure working capital and expand their operations more efficiently.

Peer-to-peer lending platforms are an emerging force in this transformation, gradually enabling SMEs to access funding directly from a network of individual and institutional investors. These platforms allow SMEs to obtain loans without the delays and stringent requirements typically associated with traditional banks. By connecting businesses with multiple investors seeking high-return, short-term investments, these platforms democratise access to finance, enabling companies of all sizes to fund growth projects, manage cash flow and meet their working capital needs.

Similarly, crowdfunding platforms are emerging as powerful tools for SME financing. These platforms focus on debt and equity financing, allowing businesses to secure funds from diverse investors in exchange for shares or loan agreements. This model provides SMEs with the liquidity they need and offers investors a chance to participate in the growth of promising enterprises. These non-banking platforms are critical in addressing the $123 billion SME financing gap in the MENA region, with Saudi Arabia benefiting from their ability to enhance capital access and support the broader economic diversification agenda.

In parallel, private equity and asset management companies are increasingly important in providing SMEs with private debt and alternative financing solutions. These firms focus on receivables financing and factoring, allowing businesses to unlock liquidity from their unpaid invoices and receivables. By offering structured finance arrangements, these firms are beginning to provide SMEs with flexible financing solutions tailored to their needs, complementing existing bank and government-supported initiatives like Kafalah. This form of financing is precious for businesses that operate in sectors with long payment cycles or require significant upfront capital for expansion.

These non-banking entities are starting to integrate innovative technologies such as digital platforms, blockchain and AI to streamline processes, reduce costs and increase transparency, with further potential for adoption as the market matures. For example, by digitising trade documents and automating risk assessments, these companies are enhancing the overall efficiency of the financing process, enabling faster decision-making and reducing the risks associated with cross-border transactions.

The rise of non-bank financing in Saudi Arabia represents a significant shift in how businesses access finance, complementing traditional banking services and expanding options for SMEs. These suppliers drive financial inclusion by offering more flexible and accessible options for companies traditionally underserved by the banking sector. As the Kingdom continues to push forward with its Vision 2030 goals, these non-banking platforms are expected to play an even more prominent role, helping SMEs to grow, innovate and contribute to the diversification of the Saudi economy. By bridging the financing gap, they are reshaping the trade finance ecosystem and ensuring that businesses of all sizes have the support they need to succeed in an increasingly competitive global market.

Regulatory and government support

Saudi Arabia's government has taken substantial steps to create an environment conducive to foreign investment, particularly in the trade finance sector. Through initiatives such as government-backed guarantees, capital market reforms and the promotion of a developing fintech ecosystem, the Kingdom is steadily positioning itself as an attractive destination for international investors.

Saudi Arabia has significantly improved its business environment, simplifying processes for foreign investors. The Ministry of Investment, which integrates the functions of the former SAGIA, streamlines licensing and investment procedures, providing a centralised platform for foreign companies to enter the Saudi market.

Finally, Saudi Arabia's legal framework is evolving to offer robust investor protections, exemplified by the Bankruptcy Law (2018), which introduces a more transparent process for debt recovery, enhancing the security of the receivables financing sector. This legislation provides a more transparent process for debt recovery in cases of default, thereby creating a more secure environment for creditors and further supporting the growth of the receivables financing sector. These policies contribute to a stable and attractive investment climate, helping Saudi Arabia emerge as a competitive destination for international trade finance and receivables investment.

As Saudi Arabia continues to enhance its trade finance eco-system, opportunities for foreign investors are multiplying. International companies can partner with local firms to access the Saudi market, leveraging government incentives, including sector-specific tax breaks, duty exemptions and strong investment protections.

Saudi's favourable taxation environment

Saudi Arabia's taxation environment offers significant advantages for investors, particularly in receivable financing, contributing to its attractiveness as a global hub and not only for trade finance. At the time of writing, a notable aspect of the Kingdom's tax regime is the absence of personal income tax, allowing local and foreign investors to retain 100 per cent of their earnings. Additionally, foreign investors enjoy significant tax advantages, including exemptions on capital gains for qualifying financial investments. This makes receivable financing an attractive avenue under the Kingdom's tax regime. Corporations' corporate tax rate is a flat 20 per cent on profits. In contrast, Zakat, a religious tax, is primarily applicable to Saudi and GCC nationals and their businesses, while foreign-owned entities benefit from the standard corporate tax framework, further enhancing the appeal for international investors. This creates a favourable tax environment for foreign-owned entities, including factoring companies.

Profit repatriation in Saudi Arabia is streamlined and investor-friendly, with minimal restrictions. Withholding taxes on certain payments to non-residents may apply but are mitigated by Saudi Arabia's extensive network of Double Taxation Avoidance Treaties (DTAs). Saudi Arabia has also established over 50 Double Taxation Avoidance Treaties (DTAs) with critical markets such as the US, UK and Germany, preventing double taxation of income and capital gains. This makes cross-border investments in receivable financing even more appealing.

Regarding trade incentives, the GCC Common External Tariff framework fosters tariff-free or low-tariff trade within GCC countries. This streamlined regional trade environment creates a fertile ground for receivable financing opportunities. Moreover, government-backed programs like Kafalah and the Saudi Export-Import Bank (EXIM) are essential in providing loan guarantees and export credit insurance, significantly reducing risk for investors in receivable financing. Saudi Arabia's regulatory framework supports interest rate flexibility, empowering factoring companies to tailor financing terms directly with their clients while aligning with the Kingdom's financial and Sharia principles.

Saudi Arabia shows what trade financing is capable of

Saudi Arabia's journey through Vision 2030 is not merely a reflection of regional ambition – it is a testament to the power of trade finance as a driver of economic transformation. This chapter has illuminated how the Kingdom's diversification strategy is shaped by a dynamic ecosystem of private lenders, fund managers and innovative financial solutions working alongside government initiatives to create lasting change. Private actors are not just participants in this landscape – they are the catalysts enabling cross-border trade, supporting SMEs and driving the financial innovation that will define Saudi Arabia's future.

The transformation of Saudi Arabia, particularly in its trade finance sector, is about much more than domestic growth. It reflects a broader, global narrative where trade finance is pivotal in reshaping economies and securing long-term sustainability. The Kingdom's focus on building a modern financial infrastructure, backed by digitalisation and cross-border connectivity, is creating a platform for innovation that will influence the flow of global trade for years to come. Saudi Arabia is becoming a key player in this evolving story of international trade finance and its experience offers a compelling example of how strategic reforms can pivot an entire economy.

This is more than just a success story for Saudi Arabia: It is a microcosm of what trade finance can achieve on a larger scale – facilitating economic diversification, enhancing global integration and providing a pathway for other emerging markets. The Kingdom is positioning itself as a laboratory for financial innovation, offering valuable lessons on how digitalisation, supply chain finance and private capital can drive sustainable growth in an increasingly interconnected world.

Trade Works

For those observing the Kingdom's rise, there is something uniquely compelling about how Saudi Arabia's journey speaks to the future of global trade. This is not about fleeting trends or short-term gains. Instead, it's about creating a resilient, diversified economy equipped to thrive in the post-oil world – where trade finance opportunities stretch beyond borders and traditional industries. In many ways, Saudi Arabia stands as a masterclass in how modern economies can harness trade finance to redefine their economic landscapes, providing insight into the future of global trade.

Ultimately, the Kingdom's story is not just about the present – it's about the potential for trade finance to shape a new era of global commerce. Whether you're a financial strategist, an observer of emerging markets or someone interested in how economies evolve, Saudi Arabia's experience offers invaluable lessons. The interplay of private innovation, government-backed initiatives and global integration in the Kingdom is setting the stage for a new chapter in international trade finance that will undoubtedly influence the next frontier of investment and economic development.

Chapter 10:

Opportunities: How to Invest in Trade Financing

T rade financing involves multiple components and often requires significant capital, which may seem risky at first glance. However, trade finance remains one of the most secure investment opportunities, even during periods of stock-market volatility.

In the post-pandemic recovery, trade financing has emerged as a critical pillar in revitalising global commerce. The increasing reliance on digital platforms, driven by advancements in block-chain technology and artificial intelligence, has revolutionised how transactions are conducted – making them faster, more transparent and more secure. This digital transformation has been instrumental in mitigating risks traditionally associated with trade finance, providing a more resilient and efficient solution for businesses navigating the complexities of global trade. As companies worldwide adopt these innovations, trade finance continues to play a key role in fostering economic growth across both developed and emerging markets.

So why has this asset class not yet attracted more investors? This chapter explores the various ways to invest in trade finance without needing to establish a company dedicated to this business model.

Trade finance as a compelling asset class

Despite its unique advantages, trade financing remains an underrepresented asset class in investor portfolios. Uncorrelated to the stock market, trade finance receives limited attention from analysts and researchers. As banks reduce their role in financing global SME trade, the demand for alternative sources of capital continues to grow, particularly in emerging industries. Trade finance offers better and faster returns than traditional investments like stocks or bonds.

The trade-financing gap has been exacerbated by several factors: the ongoing rejection of trade finance applications by large banks, regulatory changes following the global financial crisis, and the challenges posed by the COVID-19 pandemic. Despite these hurdles, trade finance has shown remarkable resilience despite global economic volatility, including geo-political tensions and evolving trade policies, particularly between significant economies such as the USA and China. Data from 2023 highlights this resilience: while global trade flows faced substantial disruptions, the trade finance sector remained robust, underpinned by its adaptability and critical role in maintaining supply chains. The ICC's 2023 Trade Register underscored the stability of trade finance assets, even as geopolitical risks increased, reaffirming its value as a secure investment in uncertain times.

Geopolitical tensions and trade sanctions continue to shape the trade finance landscape. The US and other nations impose major sanctions on countries like Iran and China, while China enacts retaliatory measures. Despite these complexities, trade finance accounts for approximately 90 per cent of global trade, leaving substantial opportunities for investors interested in bridging the financing gap between SMEs and suppliers.

In recent years, non-banking financial institutions (NBFIs) have become increasingly vital in providing liquidity to SMEs, particularly as traditional banks tighten lending regulations. NBFIs – including fintech companies, private equity firms and insurance providers – are offering more flexible and innovative financing solutions, leveraging technology to streamline the process and make financing more accessible to smaller businesses. This shift supports the growth of SMEs and presents a significant opportunity for investors to tap into a resilient and expanding market.

Trade finance falls within the broader category of private debt, providing capital to businesses upfront under agreed repayment terms. It can take various forms, depending on the specific needs of the SMEs, the type of market they operate in and whether they are importing or exporting goods. However, the lack of easily digestible information often prevents many investors from engaging with trade finance, as they may be hesitant to invest in something they need help understanding.

Trade requires both a seller and a buyer, but the capital needed to facilitate the transaction often comes from a third party. Private lenders provide a feasible and modern solution for SMEs that lack sufficient capital. Trade financing is highly collateralised, making it a more secure investment than other financial assets. Trade finance resembles a fixed-income product, as it falls under the private debt category rather than equity.

Trade finance as an inflation hedge and strategic investment choice

In the current economic environment, characterised by enduring inflation and capricious markets, investors are in a perpetual quest for strategies that preserve their capital and deliver sustainable growth. Traditional investment havens, such as gold and real estate, while historically lauded for their economic downturn resilience, now might suffer challenges that detract from their appeal.

Gold, for its part, despite being a steadfast value repository, does not generate income through dividends or interest, drawing on cash reserves for storage and insurance. Real estate, though potentially lucrative, demands considerable management effort. It is beset with high transaction costs and marred by liquidity constraints, rendering it a less attractive option for those pursuing flexibility and prompt returns.

Against this backdrop, trade finance – a subset of private debt – emerges as an appealing yet century-old alternative investment strategy, offering a novel solution to the inflation conundrum.

The following remarks seek to unravel the essence of trade finance, its mechanisms, its viability as an inflation hedge, the pivotal role of credit insurance and the strategic considerations in selecting appropriate trade finance funds, thereby charting a course for investors to harness low volatility through premium fixed-income returns.

The appeal of trade finance in inflationary times

Inflation, a scourge on purchasing power, can destabilise investment portfolios. Trade finance, however, exemplifies resilience. The inherent connection of trade finance to tangible goods and the tangible economy ensures that as prices increase, the value of transactions facilitated by trade finance also rises. This direct correlation provides a natural inflation hedge, safeguarding investors' capital from the despoliations of increasing prices.

Moreover, the typically short duration of trade finance agreements affords rapid turnover, granting investors agility in adapting to market shifts. A critical advantage in an inflationary milieu. Warren Buffet's forays into leading Japanese trading houses underscore trade finance's potential, yielding meaningful returns, confirming it as a strategic and valid investment choice.

The role of credit insurance in trade finance

Credit insurance, a crucial facet of trade finance, diminishes non-payment risk by covering a transaction's value in the event of a buyer default, thus reducing exporters' exposure to their trading partners' economic instability and enabling more confident credit term extensions. For investors, it translates into a more secure investment proposition. Credit insurance is instrumental in the trade finance ecosystem, safeguarding against the vagaries of cross-border transactions.

Selecting the right trade finance special purpose vehicle (SPV)

Investment in trade finance demands discernment. The selection of an appropriate trade finance fund necessitates a comprehensive evaluation of its risk-management strategies, its adeptness at navigating international trade intricacies and the transparency and allure of its terms.

Investors should gravitate toward investment vehicles that demonstrate profound trade finance acumen, rigorous due diligence and competitive returns. An astutely chosen trade finance fund can be a cornerstone of a diversified investment portfolio, offering stable income and enhancing liquidity while mitigating risk.

Impact investing and economic contributions

Trade finance transcends mere investment, serving as a conduit for impact investing. By channelling capital toward international trade facilitation, investors contribute to economic development, especially in emerging markets where financing access is paramount. Addressing a $2.6 trillion global trade finance gap yields financial returns. It catalyses positive societal change, bolstering SMEs and the economic spine of any society, creating jobs and economic resilience.

Definitely a recommendable addition to an investor's portfolio

As investors navigate through the turbulent seas of the global economy, trade finance stands as a beacon of stability and growth. Its unique amalgamation of risk mitigation, liquidity and tangible economic activity connection positions it as an exemplary inflation hedge. Trades are enhanced by credit insurance and trade finance beckons as a compelling choice for those aiming to diversify their portfolios while contributing to worldwide economic advancement, epitomising innovation and opportunity in strategies designed to counter inflation's challenges.

Searching for a suitable benchmark for trade finance funds

Correct benchmarking is crucial before selecting and investing in a fund, as it validates past performance against comparable investments. Many trade finance funds fail because they do not use comparable benchmarks. Consequently, critical investors disregard a relatively low-volatility and low-risk asset class, missing a unique niche investment opportunity.

Our recent in-house research at Artis found that none of the trade finance funds we examined currently benchmark against a private debt index, which we consider a better fit than a public debt index that follows other criteria.

To clarify the distinction, a *private debt index* tracks the performance of loans made to private companies that are not publicly traded, such as stocks or government bonds. These loans are typically part of direct agreements with companies rather than being listed on public markets. A private debt index includes loans or credit extended to private entities through direct lending, mezzanine financing, distressed debt and other private lending structures. These investments are often less liquid and not traded on public exchanges.

In contrast, a *public debt index* comprises bonds issued by governments or publicly traded corporations, such as US Treasury bonds or German Bonds. These bonds are traded on stock exchanges and typically have lower risk and return profiles than private debt instruments.

When evaluating trade finance funds, examining the benchmarks they use is crucial. Public debt indices are often employed but are usually inappropriate for trade finance, while private debt indices provide a much more suitable comparison. By aligning with a comparable risk-return profile, better-selected benchmarks improve the analysis and assessment of a fund's performance, ultimately increasing investor understanding and confidence in the trade finance sector.

Common benchmarks and their shortcomings

Most trade finance funds use straight benchmarks such as central bank interest rates or public debt indices. However, trade finance funds invest in financial instruments such as letters of credit, often combined with (export) credit insurance, which, in addition to producing a yield, smooth the exchange of goods and services and mitigate risks like non- or late payment, features that are not included in a straight interest-producing asset.

Trade investments often generate an equity-like yield from a trading margin, not interest, rendering interest-rate-based benchmarks less comparable; yields from private debt investments are a more appropriate comparison. Any index that includes public debt – such as leveraged loans, high-yield bonds or money market funds – is also irrelevant because trade finance does not deal with such vehicles.

In today's interest rate scenario, benchmarking a fund to interest rates or public debt means comparing a 14 per cent to 20 per cent per annum trade finance investment yield in the private debt sector with a 4 per cent to 8 per cent return in the public debt index. Investors might find such comparisons confusing or inappropriate and might need more confidence.

What could a bespoke benchmark look like for trade finance?

Let's explore more suitable benchmarking solutions, such as a bespoke benchmark. A bespoke benchmark is a custom index explicitly designed for a particular investment strategy or asset class, such as trade finance. It allows for a more accurate comparison of volatility and performance in your trade finance fund.

While this would provide an accurate view of risk and return, it will not give the investors a validated or familiar index they can trust and feel comfortable with. Customised benchmarks are often complex to compile as sourcing the data might be expensive and require subscriptions to multiple specialist providers.

Why is a familiar index important for investor confidence?

Benchmarking against a well-known equity index such as the S&P 500 could be another way to familiarise oneself with the index. However, the risk-return profile in equity indices does not relate well to any private debt investments; trade finance is a subset.

Many trade finance funds enjoy lower volatility than other asset classes, including equities and many parts of the public debt market. To illustrate, in market crashes such as the global financial crisis 2008, where the stock market experienced a severe downturn, trade finance funds were generally much less affected than equity funds and behaved better during volatile periods. Trade finance is not comparable with private equity benchmarks, either.

This combination of premium returns and low downside risk gives trade finance funds strong potential for investors. The challenge is to find a benchmark that provides confidence – a validated index that compares accurately.

Are private debt benchmarks the better choice?

After careful analysis, private debt benchmarks emerge as the best fit for trade finance funds. These indices have loan and risk-return profiles that closely resemble those of trade finance funds. They are 'private sector-related', meaning they primarily consist of loans and investments made in the private sector without exposure to public debt.

For example, one private debt index returned around 12 per cent in 2023 and 9 per cent on average over the past five years, providing a more accurate comparison to trade finance investments. While some trade finance funds have outperformed private debt indices, others haven't.

With private debt indexes providing more accuracy in bench-marking, why trade funds haven't used private debt indices and instead used less appropriate benchmarks remains open for speculation.

Be this as it may, using less relevant comparisons undermines investor confidence regardless of the investment sector or asset class.

A more appropriate benchmark provides more transparency and confidence in the market and the asset class.

Conclusion

Trade finance funds or other investment vehicles present a compelling investment opportunity, mainly when backed by credit insurance. Some funds in this sector offer stable, double-digit returns with lower risk than other debt markets, thanks to collateralised transactions and trading with reliable counter-parties. The true appeal of trade finance as an asset class only becomes evident when evaluated against a suitable benchmark.

I hope this book has effectively highlighted the advantages of investing in trade finance and provided a deeper understanding of its potential.

Glossary

AI	Artificial intelligence
AML	Anti-money laundering
B2B	Business-to-business (lending platforms) – see P2P
BA	Bankers' acceptance, a specific type of bill of exchange used since the beginning of the trade by international merchants to finance their trade activities
BaFin	Federal Financial Supervisory Authority, Germany (*Bundesanstalt für Finanzdienstleistungsaufsicht*)
Basel regulations	The Basel Regulations are a set of international regulations developed by the Basel Committee on Banking Supervision. Their main aim is to stabilise the international financial system through a regulatory framework.
Big data	Extremely large data sets which reveal patterns, trends and associations when analysed by a computer
BG	Bank guarantee, a financial instrument issued by a bank that guarantees that an agreed-upon amount will be paid to a financier at an agreed-upon date

Bill of lading	A specific cargo or lot of goods has already been financed and is already allocated to a destination.
Blockchain	A digital ledger in which transactions are recorded across an entire network of computers that are interconnected. The goal behind such a ledger is to ensure that the system cannot be hacked into.
CBR	Correspondent banking relationship
CHF	Swiss francs
Cryptocurrency	A digital currency in which cryptography is used for transactions which are verified and records are maintained by a decentralised system.
DeFi	Decentralised finance
Disintermediation	Using fewer intermediaries in a transaction
DLT	Distributed ledger technology
DPO	Days payable outstanding (the average number of days it takes for a company to pay its suppliers and a benchmark for investor and financing companies to determine the creditworthiness of a business).
ESG	Environmental, social and governance
ESR	Environmental and socially responsible standards
Factoring	Buying an invoice from an exporter at a discount and receiving the payment from that invoice by the importer on a pre-agreed future date
FATF	Financial Action Task Force

FCA	Financial Conduct Authority (UK)
FINMA	Financial Market Supervisory Authority (Switzerland)
Fintech	Financial technology, which is the integration of technology in the provision of financial services by a company. The goal is to bring about innovation and provide improved services to clients.
FMCG	Fast-moving consumer goods
GDP	Gross domestic product
GFC	Global Financial Crisis
ICC	International Chamber of Commerce, the world's business organization, HQ in Paris. Represents 45 million companies in over 170 countries.
IMF	International Monetary Fund
IoT	Internet of things – the network of interrelated devices that connect and exchange data
KYC	Know Your Customer or Know Your Client
Large cap	Large companies with a market cap of between $10 billion to $200 billion. These are usually large stocks that prove to be more stable and are therefore preferred by investors.
LC	Letter of credit, which is the obligation of a bank to pay upon completion and confirmation of pre-agreed contractual terms
Loss payee	The party to whom the claim from a loss is to be paid.
OECD	Organisation for Economic Co-operation and Development

Open account	Goods are shipped and delivered before the payment is due
P2P	Peer-to-peer (lending platforms) – see B2B
Panama Papers	Leaked financial documents that mention details of tens of thousands offshore entities where a former Panama law firm – Mossack Fonseca – was particularly active
Paradise Papers	Leaked details of offshore service providers that were obtained by the German newspaper *Süddeutsche Zeitung*. These papers revealed financial activities of politicians, corporations, world leaders and celebrities from all over the world
Ponzi scheme	A fraud in which investors are led to believe in the success of a non-existent enterprise by the payment of quick returns to the previous investors from money invested later
PPP	Paycheck Protection Program
Protected default	Ensures that all claims clauses are settled within six months, regardless of the jurisdiction
Purchase and sale	The financing party replaces the buyer and takes ownership of the asset finance
Repo	Repurchase agreement
SCF	Supply chain financing
SDN list	Specially Designated Nationals and Blocked Persons list (US)
Skonto	Discount
SME	Small and medium-sized enterprise

Sōgō shōsha	Large Japanese conglomerates which trade across many platforms
SPV	Special Purchase Vehicle
SRI	Socially responsible investing
Standstill	Capital controls introduced for banks in Europe in 1931
Tenor	The number of calendar days until maturity of a trade
Trade Repo	Trade Repurchase Agreement. The purpose is to borrow agreement money instantly. One party sells an asset to another party at one price and commits to repurchase the same or another part of the same asset from the second party at a different price at a future date or on demand.
UBO	Ultimate beneficial owner
WTO	World Trade Organization

Sources

Accominotti, O., 'London merchant banks, the central European panic, and the sterling crisis of 1931', *Journal of Economic History*, 72 (I) (2012), pp.1–43.

Anonymous, 'Are You a Robot? Bloomberg Investigates, *AI & Machine Learning* (16 Dec. 2021). See also https://aimltechbrief.com/index.php/news/item/7646-are-you-a-robot-bloomberg-investigates; accessed 22 Mar. 2025.

Anonymous, 'Risk & Compliance Glossary: What are Dual-Use Goods?' *Dow Jones, News Corp.* See also www.dowjones.com/professional/risk/glossary/dual-use-goods-definition/; accessed 21 Mar. 2025.

Anonymous, Trade Credit vs. Trade Finance: What's the Difference?' *Niche Trade Credit.* See also https://nichetc.com.au/trade-credit-vs-trade-finance-whats-the-difference/; accessed 17 Mar. 2025.

Anonymous, 'Trade Finance Funds Grow as Investors Seek "Recession-Proof" Asset Class', *S&P Global* (04 Nov. 2019). See also https://thriver.finance/wp-content/uploads/2021/03/Trade-finance-funds-grow-as-investors-seek-recession-proof-asset-class-II-3.pdf; accessed 23 Mar. 2025.

Artis Trade Invest; See also https://artistradeinvest.com/; accessed 07 Sep. 2021.

Bank for International Settlements (BIS), 'The Basel Committee - Overview', *BIS.* 2021. See also www.bis.org/bcbs/index.htm?m=88; accessed 17 Mar. 2025.

—— 'History - Overview', *BIS* (09 Nov. 2020). See also www.bis.org/about/history.htm?m=13; accessed 22 Mar. 2025.

Basquill, John, 'Legal Roundtable: Learning Lessons from Trade Finance Fraud', *Global Trade Review* (21 Jan. 2020).

——'Money Laundering Groups "Exploiting Trade Finance Transactions", Task Force Warns', *Global Trade Review* (09 Dec. 2020).

Beattie, Andrew, 'How Did Nick Leeson Contribute to the Fall of Barings Bank?' *Investopedia* (18 Dec. 2022).

Carvajo, Marco, '5 Facts You Need to Know About Trade Finance', *The Balance* (09 Dec. 2019). See also www.thebalancemoney.com/trade-finance-explained-5-facts-you-need-to-know-3953592; accessed 22 Mar. 2025.

Chanjaroen, Chanyaporn, Alfred Cang and Lulu Yilun Chen, 'After $9 Billion Credit Hit, Banks Seek Trade Finance Revamp', *Bloomberg, Technology* (09 Jul. 2020).

Chen, James, 'Know Your Client (KYC): What it Means and Compliance Requirements', *Investopedia* (06 Aug. 2024). See also www.investopedia.com/terms/k/knowyourclient.asp; accessed 22 Mar. 2025.

Craig, Ben R., 'The Souk al-Manakh Crash', *Federal Reserve Bank of Cleveland, Economic Commentary 2019-20.* (18 Nov. 2019) See also www.clevelandfed.org/publications/economic-commentary/ec-201920-kuwait-souk-al-manakh; accessed 22 Mar. 2025.

Dann, Clarissa, 'Trade Finance and the Blockchain – Three Essential Case Studies', *Flow, Deutsche Bank,* Dec. 2017. See also https://flow.db.com/trade-finance/trade-finance-and-the-blockchain-three-essential-case-studies; accessed 22 Mar. 2025.

Denton, John, 'Letter: Small Business Needs the G20 to Safeguard Trade Financing', *Financial Times* (17 Nov. 2020).

De Paoli, Lucca and Nabila Ahmed, 'Greensill's Swift Fall was Triggered by Insurer Who Balked', *Bloomberg News* (03 Mar. 2021).

Federal Bureau of Investigation (FBI), 'Firearms Checks (National Incidence Criminal Background Check System (NICS)', *FBI.* See also www.fbi.gov/how-we-can-help-you/more-fbi-services-and-information/nics; accessed 22 Mar. 2025.

Federal Reserve Banks, '2019 Report on Employer Firms: Based on the 2018 Small Business Credit Survey', *Small Business Credit Survey,* 2019.

Financial Action Task Force (FATF) and Egmont Group, 'Trade-based Money Laundering Trends and Developments', *FATF/OECD and Egmont Group of Financial Intelligence Units,* Dec. 2020.

Global Trade Review (GTR), 'How Trade Finance Can Join the Dots on ESG', (19 Apr. 2021). See also www.gtreview.com/magazine/volume-19-issue-2/trade-finance-can-join-dots-esg/; accessed 22 Mar. 2025.

Greenwald, John, 'A Very Special Recession', *TIME* 122 *(23)* (28 Nov. 1983). See also https://time.com/archive/6860262/a-very-special-recession/; accessed 21 Mar. 2025.

Hayes, Adam. 'Short Straddle: Option Strategies and Examples', *Investopedia* (16 Mar. 2023). See also www.investopedia.com/terms/s/shortstraddle.asp#:~:text=A%20short%20straddle%20is%20an%20options%20trading%20strategy%20in%20which,the%20premium%20as%20a%20profit; accessed 22 Mar. 2025.

International Chamber of Commerce (ICC), '2019 ICC Trade Register Report: Global

Risks in Trade Finance', *ICC*, May 2020.

—— 'Priming Trade Finance to Safeguard SMEs and Power a Resilient

Recovery from Covid-19', *ICC* (06 Nov. 2020).

International Consortium of Investigative Journalists (ICIJ), 'About

the Paradise Papers Investigation', (05 Nov. 2017). See also www.icij.org/investigations/paradise-papers/about-the-investigation-2/; accessed 20 Mar. 2025.

International Labour Organization (ILO), 'The Power of Small: Unlocking the Potential of SMEs', *ILO*, 2019. See also https://webapps.ilo.org/infostories/en-GB/Stories/Employment/SMEs#intro; accessed 22 Mar. 2025.

International Trade Administration, U.S. Department of Commerce, 'Trade Finance Guide'. See also www.trade.gov/report/trade-finance-guide; accessed 22 Mar. 2025.

Jeffrey, Claudia, 'AI and Cryptocurrency – How They Can Work Together Effectively', *Global Trade Magazine* (16 Sep. 2020).

Kagan, Julia, 'Letter of Credit', *Investopedia*: 'Loss Payee', *Investopedia* (24.05.2024).

Karthikeyan, Sumitra, *et al.*, 'Breaking the Commodity Trap in Trade Finance', *Boston Consulting Group (BCG)* (09 Jul. 2019). See also www.bcg.com/publications/2019/breaking-commodity-trap-trade-finance; accessed 21 Mar. 2025.

Kazmi, Robert, 'AI in Fintech: Use Cases', *Koombea* (17 Sep. 2021). See also www.koombea.com/blog/ai-in-fintech/; accessed 22 Mar. 2025.

Keljikian, Sadie and David Estrakh, 'Trade Finance vs. Bank Loans Part I: Why Trade Finance?' *Express Trade Capital* (27 Jan. 2017). See also https://expresstradecapital.com/trade-finance-vs-bank-loans-part-1; accessed 22 Mar. 2025.

Lascelles, David, 'Merchant Banks No Longer Rule the City but their Influence Hasn't Gone', *City AM* (14 Nov. 2013).

Lopez, Adam, 'What Does Loss Payee Mean in Insurance Terms?' *BCS University Video Library*. 2021.

Masai, Yasuo *et al.*, 'Japan: History, Flag, Map, Population, and Facts', *Encyclopedia Britannica* (21 Mar. 2025).

Mulroy, Peter, 'View from the Top: Factoring and Credit Insurance in 2021', *Trade Finance Global* (15 Jun. 2021).

Nelson, Eshe, Jack Ewing and Liz Alderman, 'The Swift Collapse of a Company Built on Debt', *The Business Times* (29 Mar. 2021).

Obermaier, Frederik, Gerard Ryle and Bastian Obermayer, *Panama Papers*, 2016.

Organisation for Economic Co-operation and Development (OECD), 'Trade Finance for SMEs in the Digital Era', *OECD SME and Entrepreneurship Papers*, No. 24, OECD Publishing, Paris, 03 May 2021.

PYMNTS, 'Greensill: One-Off Unravelling or Hint of Supply Chain Financing Issues?' *PYMNTS* (02 Mar. 2021). See also www.pymnts.com/news/b2b-payments/2021/greensill-capital-supply-chain-financing-issues/; accessed 18 Mar. 2025.

Reuters, 'Factbox: Japan Markets and Economy after Kobe Earthquake', *Reuters* (13 Mar. 2011).

RTS Financial, 'How Factoring Builds Working Capital and Fuels Business Growth', *RTS Financial*. See also www.rtsinc.com/page/what-is-factoring-ab; accessed 07 Sep. 2021.

Ryan, Patrick, 'The Sogo Shosha – An Insider's Perspective', *Marubeni Research Institute* (28 Aug. 2013).

Schwellenbach, Nick and Ryan Summers, 'Red Flags: The First Year of COVID-19 Loan Fraud Cases', *Project on Government Oversight (POGO)* (15 Apr. 2021). See also www.pogo.org/investigations/red-flags-the-first-year-of-covid-19-loan-fraud-cases; accessed 22 Mar. 2025.

Senechal, Thierry (ed.), ICC Banking Commission, '2013 Global Risks Trade Finance Report', *ICC*, Apr. 2013.

Shimizu, Ritsuko, 'Japan's Mitsubishi Corp Targets Majority Stake in Lawson', *Reuters* (15 Sep. 2016); See also www.reuters.com/article/us-lawson-m-a-mitsubishi/japans-mitsubishi-corp-targets-majority-stake-in-lawson-idUSKCN11L0A7 accessed 22 Mar. 2025.

Simmons & Simmons JWS, 'FinTech in Trade and Trade Finance', (14 Dec. 2016).

Smith, Hedrick, 'Is Wal-Mart Good for America?' (transcript, video) Season 2004, Ep. 16, *FRONTLINE, Public Broadcasting Service (PBS)* (16 Nov. 2004). See also www.pbs.org/wgbh/pages/frontline/shows/walmart/etc/script.html

https://video.pbsnc.org/video/frontline-wal-mart-good-america/; accessed 23 Mar. 2025.

Smith, Robert, 'SoftBank-backed Greensill Suffers Raft of Client Defaults', *Financial Times* (04 May 2020).

Tanaka, Takayuki, 'Research on Sogo Shosha: Origins, Establishment, and Development', *Japan Foreign Trade Council (JFTC)*, Oct. 2012.

Tardi, Carla, 'Value Chains: Definition, Model, Analysis, and Example, *Investopedia* (30 Jul. 2024). See also www.investopedia.com/terms/v/valuechain.asp; accessed 24 Mar. 2025.

Trade Finance Global, 'Receivables Finance 2025 Guide', *Trade Finance Global* (30 Jan. 2025). See also www.tradefinanceglobal.com/receivables-finance/; accessed 23 Mar. 2025.

Board of Governors of the Federal Reserve System, 'About the Fed'. See also www.federalreserve.gov/aboutthefed.htm; accessed 14 Nov. 2024.

Yep, Eric, 'After Hin Leong: Collapse of a Singaporean Oil Prodigy', *S&P Global* (24 Sep. 2020).

Zaldokas, Alminas and Emilio Bisetti, 'Supplying Finance to Supply Chains', *South China Morning Post* (15 Jul 2021).

Index

www.ingramcontent.com/pod-product-compliance
Lightning Source LLC
Chambersburg PA
CBHW071554210326
41597CB00019B/3239